Home Folks' Old-Fashioned

SLOW-COOKER RECIPES

SWEETWATER
PRESS

Home Folks' Old-Fashioned Slow-Cooker Recipes

Copyright © 2006 Sweetwater Press

Produced by Cliff Road Books

ISBN-13: 978-1-58173-594-9
ISBN-10: 1-58173-594-4

Design by Miles G. Parsons

Printed in China

Home Folks' Old-Fashioned

SLOW-COOKER
RECIPES

SWEETWATER
PRESS

CONTENTS

APPETIZERS

BACON ONION DIP

6 slices bacon, finely chopped
1 (8-ounce) package light cream cheese, softened
1 cup light sour cream
1/2 cup cheddar cheese, shredded
2 green onions, finely chopped
potato chips or crackers

In a non-stick skillet over medium-high heat, cook bacon 7 to 8 minutes or until crisp. Transfer to a paper towel-lined plate to drain. Place all ingredients, except bacon, in a slow cooker. Crumble the bacon and sprinkle on top. Cover and cook on high for 1 hour or until cheese is melted (do not stir). Reduce heat to low until ready to serve.

ENCHILADA DIP

2 pounds boneless, skinless chicken thighs
1 (10-ounce) can enchilada sauce
2 (8-ounce) packages cream cheese, softened
4 cups Pepper Jack cheese, shredded

Combine chicken and enchilada sauce in a slow cooker. Cover and cook on low for 8 to 10 hours, or until chicken is thoroughly cooked. Using two forks, shred chicken in the sauce.

Cut cream cheese into cubes and stir into the slow cooker, along with the cheddar cheese; mix well. Cover and cook on low for 30 minutes, stirring twice, until mixture is blended and cheese is melted.

CHILI CON QUESO

1 pound Mexican or plain pasteurized processed cheese spread
1-1/3 cups chunky salsa
1 (4-ounce) can chopped green chilies, drained
1/4 teaspoon pepper

Combine all ingredients in a slow cooker. Cover and cook on low for 2 to 2-1/2 hours or until cheese is melted, stirring twice during cooking. Remove the lid from the slow cooker and cook on high for 1 hour longer, until mixture is hot.

CHILI DIP

1 large bottle picante sauce, medium
2 cans refried beans
1 pint sour cream
1/2 teaspoon chili powder
1 pound ground beef, cooked
1 medium onion, chopped
salt and pepper to taste
1 cup cheddar cheese, shredded
jalapeños, to taste

Combine all ingredients in a slow cooker and cook 4 to 6 hours on low. Serve with raw vegetables or chips.

Spinach and Artichoke Dip

1 cup Mozzarella cheese, shredded
1 (8-ounce) package cream cheese, cubed
1/2 cup Parmesan cheese, grated
1 teaspoon garlic powder
1/4 teaspoon pepper
1 (14-ounce) can artichoke hearts, drained and chopped
1 cup spinach, chopped
1/2 cup red bell pepper, chopped
tortilla chips

Combine all ingredients in a slow cooker. Cover and cook on high for 2 hours, or until cheeses are melted. Serve with tortilla chips.

Beef Dip

1 pound ground beef
1 cup onion, chopped
1/2 cup green bell pepper, chopped
2 garlic cloves, minced
3 cups grated Monterey Jack cheese
1/2 cup chili peppers, chopped
2 teaspoons Worcestershire sauce
1 cup tomato sauce
1/2 teaspoon chili powder
tortilla chips

In a large non-stick skillet, combine beef, onion, bell pepper, and garlic. Cook over medium heat until beef is browned. Pour into a slow cooker and add the rest of the ingredients. Stir well, cover, and cook on low for 2 hours. Serve with tortilla chips.

CRAB DIP

2 (8-ounce) packages cream cheese, softened and cubed
1/4 cup sour cream
2 teaspoons Worcestershire sauce
1/4 cup green onions, sliced
2 (6-1/2-ounce) cans crabmeat, drained
crackers

Combine all ingredients in a slow cooker. Cover and cook on high until cheese melts, about 30 minutes. Stir well. Serve with crackers.

TURKEY AND CHEESE DIP

1-1/4 pounds ground turkey
1-1/4 pounds hot Italian turkey sausage, casings removed
1 pound processed cheese, cubed
1 (11-ounce) can sliced jalapeño peppers, drained
1 medium onion, finely chopped
1/2 pound cheddar cheese, cubed
8 ounces cream cheese, cubed
8 ounces cottage cheese
8 ounces sour cream
1 (8-ounce) can diced tomatoes, drained
3 medium garlic cloves, minced
salt and freshly ground black pepper, to taste
crisp crackers and tortilla chips

In a large skillet, over medium heat, cook and stir ground turkey and sausage until cooked through and all traces of pink have disappeared. Drain and transfer to a large slow cooker. Add processed cheese, jalapeños, onion, cheddar and cream cheeses, cottage cheese, sour cream, tomatoes, and garlic. Stir all ingredients in slow cooker set on high. Add salt and pepper and cook, covered, for 1-1/2 to 2 hours or until cheeses are melted. Serve with crackers and tortilla chips.

This recipe used by permission of the National Turkey Federation.

Salsa

12 small tomatoes, cored and chopped
3 garlic cloves
1 onion, chopped
2 jalapeño peppers
1/2 cup cilantro, chopped
3/4 teaspoon salt
tortilla chips

In a slow cooker, combine the tomatoes, garlic, onion, and jalapeño peppers. Cover and cook on high for 2-1/2 hours, or until tomatoes are soft. Remove from heat and let cool. Spoon the mixture into a food processor or blender. Add the cilantro and salt; blend until smooth. Serve with tortilla chips.

Marinara Sauce

2 onions, chopped
8 garlic cloves, minced
4 (14-ounce) cans diced tomatoes with Italian seasoning, undrained
1 (6-ounce) can tomato paste
1/2 cup water
2 teaspoons dried Italian seasoning

Combine all ingredients in a slow cooker, cover, and cook on low for 8 to 10 hours. Serve over pasta or as a dip for garlic bread, bread sticks, or cheese sticks.

BOILED PEANUTS

2 pounds fresh peanuts, uncooked and in shells
1/2 cup salt

Fill a slow cooker with peanuts. Cover with water and add salt; stir. Cover and cook on low for 12 to 18 hours, or until peanuts are soft. Drain and serve.

SPICY CHICKEN WINGS

2 cups brown sugar
1/4 cup hot sauce
1/2 cup butter
4 tablespoons soy sauce
4 pounds chicken wings

In a saucepan, combine the brown sugar, hot sauce, butter, and soy sauce. Heat until butter is melted. Put the chicken wings in a slow cooker and pour sauce over top. Cover and cook on low for 4 to 5 hours.

KIELBASA SAUSAGE

2 (16-ounce) packages kielbasa sausage, cut into 1-inch pieces
2 cups grape jelly
2 cups ketchup

In a large skillet, brown the sausage over medium-high heat. Meanwhile, combine the jelly and ketchup in a slow cooker. Cook on medium until combined, stirring occasionally. Add the kielbasa and reduce the heat to low. Cover and cook for 1 hour.

SWEET AND SOUR MEATBALLS

2 pounds precooked frozen meatballs
1 cup grape jelly
2 cups cocktail sauce

Heat meatballs in oven as directed on package. Place in a slow cooker. Mix jelly and cocktail sauce thoroughly, pour over meatballs, stir well, cover slow cooker, and heat on high 1 to 2 hours until sauce is hot.

Turn heat to low until ready to serve, stirring occasionally.

Party Mix

3 cups thin pretzel sticks
2 cups wheat cereal
2 cups rice cereal
3 cups mixed nuts
1 teaspoon seasoned salt
1 teaspoon garlic salt
1/2 cup butter, melted
1/4 cup Worcestershire sauce
2 tablespoons Parmesan cheese, grated

In a slow cooker, combine the pretzels, cereals, and nuts. In a bowl, combine the remaining ingredients and stir well. Pour into slow cooker and toss to coat. Cook, uncovered, for 2 hours, stirring frequently. Reduce heat to low and cook for another 2 hours.

SOUPS

Prima Dona Chili

2 pounds ground beef
1 onion, finely diced
3 garlic cloves, minced
1 (14-1/2-ounce) can diced tomatoes
2 (14-1/2-ounce) cans diced tomatoes, Italian-style
1 (8-ounce) can tomato sauce
1 cup water
1 (15-ounce) can kidney beans
1 (15-ounce) can pinto beans
2 tablespoons chili powder
1 tablespoon ground cumin
2 tablespoons white sugar
1 teaspoon salt
1 teaspoon ground black pepper
1 tablespoon hot pepper sauce

Brown the ground beef with the onion and garlic until the onion is clear. Place the ground beef mixture in a slow cooker. Add the remaining ingredients. Cover and cook on low for 6 to 8 hours.

BEAN AND BACON SOUP

4 slices bacon
1-1/4 cups dried beans
1 onion, chopped
3 cups water
1 package taco seasoning mix
2 (14-ounce) cans diced tomatoes, undrained

Cook bacon until crisp, drain on paper towels, and crumble. In a slow cooker, combine bacon with dried beans, onion, water, and taco seasoning mix and mix well to blend. Cover slow cooker and cook on low for 10 to 12 hours until beans are tender. Add tomatoes, stir well, and cook on low for 30 to 40 minutes longer until hot. Makes 6 servings.

POTATO CHOWDER

1 (5-ounce) package scalloped potato mix
4 cups chicken broth
2 onions, chopped
2 cups light cream
1/3 cup flour
1/8 teaspoon white pepper

In a slow cooker, combine potatoes and sauce from scalloped potato mix with chicken broth and onions. Stir well to blend. Cover and cook on low for 7 hours. In medium bowl, mix together cream and flour with a wire whisk until smooth. Stir this mixture into the slow cooker very slowly, stirring constantly. Stir until well blended. Cover and cook on low for 1 more hour, stirring occasionally, until soup thickens. Makes 5 servings.

BLACK BEAN MUSHROOM CHILI

1 pound dried black beans, rinsed
1 tablespoon extra virgin olive oil
1/4 cup mustard seeds
2 tablespoons chili powder
1-1/2 teaspoons cumin seeds, or ground cumin
1/2 teaspoon cardamom seeds, or ground cardamom
2 medium onions, coarsely chopped
1 pound mushrooms, sliced
1/2 pound tomatillos, husked, rinsed, and coarsely chopped
1/4 cup water
4-1/4 cups vegetable broth
1 (6-ounce) can tomato paste
2 tablespoons canned chipotle chilies in adobo sauce, minced
1-1/4 cups Monterey Jack cheese, grated
1/2 cup low-fat sour cream
1/2 cup fresh cilantro, chopped
2 limes, cut into wedges

Soak beans overnight in 2 quarts of water. (For a quicker method, place beans and water in a large pot and bring to a boil. Boil for 2 minutes. Remove from heat and let stand for 1 hour.) Drain beans, discarding soaking liquid. Meanwhile, combine oil, mustard seeds, chili powder, cumin, and cardamom in a Dutch oven. Place over high heat and stir until the spices sizzle, about 30 seconds. Add onions, mushrooms, tomatillos, and 1/4 cup water. Cover and cook, stirring occasionally, until vegetables are juicy, 5 to 7 minutes. Uncover and stir often until the juices evaporate and the vegetables are lightly browned, 10 to 15 minutes. Add broth, tomato paste, and chipotles (with sauce); mix well. Place the beans in a slow cooker. Pour the hot mixture over the beans. Turn heat to high. Put the lid on and cook until the beans are creamy to bite, 5 to 8 hours. To serve, ladle the chili into bowls. Garnish each serving with cheese, a dollop of sour cream, a sprinkling of cilantro, and lime wedges.

DINNER PARTY STEW

1 pound lean beef chuck, cut into 1-1/2 to 2-inch cubes
3 medium onions, sliced
1/2 cup tomato juice
1-3/4 cup beef broth
1 tablespoon sugar
1 small can mushrooms
1/2 cup sour cream

Place all ingredients except sour cream in a slow cooker. Cover and cook on low for 8 to 10 hours. Half an hour before serving, stir in sour cream.

HAMBURGER STEW

1 (10-ounce) package frozen mixed vegetables
1 pound lean ground beef or turkey, cooked and drained
1/2 cup chopped onion
1 (1-ounce) package beef stew seasoning mix
2 tablespoons all-purpose flour
3/4 cup water
1/4 cup beef broth or apple juice
1 (15-ounce) can small whole potatoes, drained and halved

Place all ingredients in a slow cooker and heat on high for 4 to 6 hours or on low 6 to 8 hours.

CHICKEN MUSHROOM STEW

6 boneless, skinless chicken breasts
2 tablespoons cooking oil
1 cup fresh mushrooms, sliced
1 medium onion, sliced
3 cups zucchini, diced
1 cup green pepper, diced
4 garlic cloves, minced
3 medium tomatoes, diced
1 (6-ounce) can tomato paste
3/4 cup water
2 teaspoons salt
1 teaspoon dried thyme

Place ingredients in a slow cooker in the order listed. Cover and cook on low for 6 to 8 hours.

COUNTRY CHICKEN STEW

4-1/2 cups chicken broth
3 pounds boneless chicken breast
1 cup medium sweet onions, diced
2 whole sweet onions, quartered
1 tablespoon butter
1/2 cup flour
2 tablespoons vegetable oil
2 cups frozen peas and carrots
salt and pepper, to taste

Place chicken broth, chicken, onions, and butter in a slow cooker. Cover and cook on high 1 hour. Whisk in flour. Add remaining ingredients and cook on low for 5 to 7 hours.

CHICKEN CHOWDER

1/2 cup carrots, chopped
1 cup skim milk
1 cup low sodium chicken broth
1/8 teaspoon white pepper
1 onion, chopped
2 garlic cloves, minced
1 potato, peeled and cubed
1/2 pound boneless, skinless chicken breasts, cut into 1-inch pieces
2 (15-ounce) cans creamed corn
1/4 cup dried potato flakes
1/2 cup Parmesan cheese, grated

Combine all ingredients except dried potato flakes and cheese in a slow cooker. Cover and cook on low for 5 to 6 hours or until potatoes are tender and chicken is thoroughly cooked. Add potato flakes and stir well to combine. Cook mixture on high, uncovered, for 5 to 10 minutes or until chowder has thickened and dried potato flakes have dissolved. Top each serving with cheese. Makes 4 servings.

PROSPECTOR'S STEW

2 to 3 large potatoes, peeled and cut into bite-sized pieces
1 pound kielbasa, sliced
2 (15-ounce) cans green beans, drained
1 small onion, quartered
1 clove garlic, minced
2 (10-1/2-ounce) cans cream of mushroom soup
1 cup cheddar cheese, shredded

Place all ingredients except cheddar cheese into a slow cooker. Cover and cook on low for 6 to 10 hours. Sprinkle with cheddar cheese before serving.

Best Bean Chili

1 pound lean ground beef, cooked and drained
1-1/2 cups onions, chopped
1 cup green bell pepper, chopped
1 teaspoon garlic, minced
2-1/2 tablespoons chili powder
1-1/2 teaspoons ground cumin
1 pound canned red kidney beans
1 pound canned pinto beans
2-1/4 pounds tomatoes, diced
2 tablespoons brown sugar
1 tablespoon unsweetened cocoa

Combine all ingredients in a slow cooker. Cover and cook on low 5 to 6 hours. Makes 6 servings.

Black Bean Chili

1 pound pork tenderloin, cubed
2 cups chunky salsa
1 (45-ounce) can black beans, rinsed and drained
1/2 cup chicken broth
1 red bell pepper, chopped
1 onion, chopped
1 teaspoon cumin
2 teaspoons chili powder
1 teaspoon dried oregano
1/4 cup sour cream

Place tenderloin in a slow cooker. Add remaining ingredients except sour cream. Cover and cook on low for 8 hours. Serve with sour cream.

BLACK BEAN SOUP WITH CHIPOTLE CHILES

1 tablespoon olive oil
2 medium red onions, chopped
1 medium red bell pepper, chopped
1 medium green bell pepper, chopped
4 garlic cloves, minced
4 teaspoons ground cumin
1 (16-ounce) package dried black beans, soaked overnight and
  drained
1 tablespoon canned chipotle chiles, chopped
7 cups hot water
2 tablespoons fresh lime juice
2 teaspoons coarse kosher salt
1/4 teaspoon ground black pepper
1 cup plain nonfat yogurt
1/2 cup seeded plum tomatoes, chopped
1/4 cup fresh cilantro, chopped

Heat olive oil in a large non-stick skillet over medium-high heat. Add onions and both bell peppers and sauté until beginning to brown, about 8 minutes. Add garlic and cumin; stir 1 minute. Transfer mixture to a slow cooker. Add beans and chipotles, then hot water. Cover and cook on high until beans are very tender, about 6 hours. Transfer 2 cups bean mixture to blender; puree until smooth. Return puree to remaining soup in slow cooker. Stir in lime juice, salt, and pepper. Ladle soup into bowls. Spoon a dollop of yogurt into each bowl. Sprinkle with tomatoes and cilantro and serve.

BEEF STEW

1/2 cup all-purpose flour
1 teaspoon paprika
salt and freshly ground pepper, to taste
2 pounds well-trimmed beef chuck, cut into 1-1/4-inch chunks
1/4 cup olive oil, divided
1 large onion, chopped
4 small onions, each cut into 6 wedges
4 garlic cloves, minced
3/4 teaspoon dried thyme, crumbled
3 bay leaves
1 (14-1/2-ounce) can beef broth, divided
1 (14-1/2-ounce) can stewed tomatoes
1-1/2 cups water
1 pound new potatoes, cut into 1-inch chunks
2 cups butternut squash, peeled, seeded, and cut into 1-inch
  chunks
2 large carrots, cut into 1/2-inch slices

In a large bowl, mix the flour, paprika, salt, and pepper. Add beef and toss until coated. Heat 2 tablespoons of the oil over medium-high heat. Cook the beef, in small batches, for 3 to 4 minutes, until lightly browned on all sides, adding additional oil as needed. Set aside the remaining seasoned flour. Reduce the heat to medium and add the chopped onion, garlic, thyme, and bay leaves. Pour in 1/4 cup of the broth and cook, scraping with a wooden spoon to loosen any browned bits in the bottom of the pan. Cook, stirring, for 3 to 4 minutes, until the onion is tender, adding additional broth if the pot becomes dry. Stir in the reserved seasoned flour and cook, stirring constantly, for 1 minute.

Place tomatoes, water, potatoes, squash, and carrots into a slow cooker. Transfer beef mixture to slow cooker. Cover and cook for 6 to 8 hours.

Beef Stew with Mushrooms

1-1/2 pounds beef stew meat
1 (10-3/4-ounce) can condensed cream of mushroom soup
1 (4-ounce) can sliced mushrooms, drained
1/2 cup beef broth
1 package dry onion soup mix

Combine all the ingredients in a slow cooker. Cover and cook for 8 to 10 hours on low or 4 to 6 hours on high.

Southwestern Beef Soup

1 pound boneless beef round, cut into thin strips
1 tablespoon vegetable oil
1 onion, chopped
2 garlic cloves, finely chopped
1 (14-ounce) can peeled tomatoes, chopped
1 cup whole kernel corn, frozen
1 (4-ounce) can diced green chiles
2 tablespoons fresh cilantro, chopped
1 cup beef broth
1/2 teaspoon ground cumin
2 corn tortillas, in strips
2 tablespoons green onion, chopped (optional)

Stir fry beef in hot oil for 2 to 3 minutes. Place all ingredients except tortilla strips and green onion into a slow cooker. Cover and cook for 6 to 8 hours on low. Place tortilla strips in soup bowls, cover with soup. Sprinkle with green onion. Makes 4 servings.

FRENCH ONION SOUP

3 large onions, sliced
2 tablespoons butter or margarine
4 cups water
6 cubes beef bouillon
1 teaspoon Worcestershire sauce
1/2 teaspoon paprika
dash of pepper

In a large frying pan, cook onions in butter until golden. Place the onion mixture in a slow cooker. Add water, bouillon cubes, Worcestershire sauce, paprika, and pepper. Cover and cook on low for 4 to 6 hours or on high for 1-1/2 to 2 hours. Serve with a slice of toasted French bread and sprinkle with Parmesan cheese, grated if desired. Makes 4 to 6 servings.

CHICKEN RICE SOUP

3 onions, chopped
4 celery stalks, sliced
salt and pepper, to taste
1 teaspoon basil
1/2 teaspoon thyme
1/2 teaspoon sage
1 (20-ounce) package frozen peas
2-1/2 pounds chicken, cut in pieces
5-1/2 cups water
3/4 cup rice, uncooked

Place all ingredients, except rice, into a slow cooker in order listed. Cover and cook 1 hour on high; reduce heat to low and cook for an additional 8 to 9 hours. One hour before serving, remove chicken and cool slightly. Remove meat from bones and return to slow cooker. Add rice. Cover and cook an additional hour on high.

FISH CHOWDER

2 celery stalks, chopped
1 green bell pepper, chopped
1 onion, chopped
3 garlic cloves, minced
2 (14-ounce) cans diced tomatoes, undrained
2 cups vegetable juice
1 cup vegetable broth or fish stock
1 tablespoon Worcestershire sauce
1/2 teaspoon salt
1/4 teaspoon crushed red pepper flakes
1 pound firm fish steaks (haddock, swordfish, halibut, salmon),
  cut into 1-inch pieces
1/2 cup instant rice, uncooked
1/4 cup fresh parsley, chopped
1 teaspoon grated lemon peel
2 tablespoons Parmesan cheese, grated

Mix all ingredients except fish, rice, parsley, lemon peel, and
Parmesan cheese in a quart slow cooker. Cover slow cooker and cook
on low for 6 to 7 hours (high setting 3 to 4 hours) until vegetables are
tender. Stir in fish and rice. Cover slow cooker and cook on high for
30 to 45 minutes until fish flakes easily when tested with a fork.

Meanwhile, in a small bowl combine parsley, lemon peel, and
cheese and mix to blend. Serve this topping with chowder. Makes 8
servings.

GREEK STEW

2 cups butternut squash, cubed
2 cups carrots, chopped
2 onions, chopped
1 cup zucchini, chopped
2 (14-ounce) cans diced tomatoes, undrained
1 (15-ounce) can garbanzo beans, rinsed and drained
1 (14-ounce) can vegetable broth
2 garlic cloves, minced
1 teaspoon cumin
1/2 teaspoon salt
1/2 teaspoon allspice
1/4 teaspoon pepper
4 cups hot cooked couscous
1/2 cup feta cheese, crumbled

Combine all ingredients except couscous and cheese in a slow cooker; mix well to combine. Cover and cook on low for 7 to 9 hours or until all vegetables are tender. Serve with couscous and sprinkle with cheese.

HAM AND LENTIL STEW

3 cups ham, cooked and chopped
3 cups carrots, chopped
2 cups dried lentils, sorted and rinsed
2 onions, chopped
2 (10-ounce) cans condensed chicken broth
4 cups water

Combine all ingredients in a slow cooker and mix to combine. Cover slow cooker and cook on low for 7 to 9 hours.

CHICKEN SOUP

1 tablespoon olive oil
1 tablespoon butter
1 pound boneless, skinless chicken thighs, chopped
2 stalks celery, with leaves, sliced
2 large carrots, sliced
1 onion, chopped
1 (14-ounce) can diced tomatoes, undrained
1 (14-ounce) can chicken broth
1 teaspoon dried thyme leaves
1/2 teaspoon salt
1/8 teaspoon pepper
1 (9-ounce) package frozen green peas
1 cup refrigerated egg noodles

Heat olive oil and butter in a skillet over medium heat. Add chicken and cook, stirring frequently, for 5 minutes. Place chicken and remaining ingredients, except peas and noodles, in a slow cooker and stir to mix. Cover slow cooker and cook on low for 6-1/2 to 7 hours, or until chicken is thoroughly cooked. Stir in peas and noodles and cook 10 minutes longer until noodles are tender and soup is thoroughly heated. Makes 8 servings.

TURKEY TORTILLA SOUP

2 skinless turkey thighs
1 pound canned tomatoes, diced
1 onion, cooked and diced
1 clove garlic, crushed
1 jalapeño pepper, seeded and chopped
4 cups chicken stock
tortilla chips
1/2 cup fresh cilantro, chopped

Combine first six ingredients and salt to taste in a slow cooker. Cover and cook on low 7 to 8 hours, until turkey is tender.

Remove turkey from slow cooker and cool slightly. Remove meat and discard bones. Chop turkey meat and divide among soup bowls. Process remaining soup mixture in a blender or food processor until puréed. Pour over turkey in soup bowls. Serve with tortilla chips and cilantro.

GREEK CHILI

1 pound ground beef, browned and drained
2 tablespoons chili powder
2 tablespoons cumin powder
3 teaspoons paprika
1 teaspoon oregano
1/4 teaspoon red pepper
1 teaspoon salt
1/4 teaspoon black pepper
1 tablespoon onion, minced
1-1/2 cups water
4 slices pita bread

Put all ingredients except pita bread in a slow cooker. Cook on high for 1-1/2 to 4 hours or on low for 3-1/2 to 6 hours. Place 1/4 cup into pita bread. Makes 4 to 6 servings.

IRISH STEW

1 cup chicken broth
1 teaspoon dried marjoram leaves
1 teaspoon dried parsley leaves
3/4 teaspoon salt
1/2 teaspoon garlic powder
1/4 teaspoon pepper
1-1/4 pounds white potatoes, peeled and cut into 1-inch pieces
1 pound lean lamb stew meat, cubed
1 (8-ounce) package frozen cut green beans
2 small leeks, cut into slices
1-1/2 cups carrots, coarsely chopped

Mix together broth, marjoram, parsley, salt, garlic powder, and pepper in a slow cooker. Add potatoes, lamb, green beans, leeks, and carrots. Cover and cook on low for 7 to 9 hours.

FIREHOUSE CHILI

3 pounds lean beef, cut into 1/4-inch pieces
2 tablespoons onion powder
1 teaspoon garlic powder
2 (8-ounce) cans tomato sauce
1/4 cup chili powder
2 tablespoons ground cumin
1 tablespoon paprika
1/4 teaspoon ground oregano
1/2 teaspoon cayenne pepper
1/2 teaspoon ground white pepper
1/2 teaspoon onion powder
1/2 teaspoon salt

Combine all ingredients in a slow cooker. Cover and cook on high for
1 hour. Reduce heat and cook on low for 4 to 6 hours.

Rustic Stew

2 to 3 pounds chicken breasts, boneless and skinless
1 tablespoon butter
2 teaspoons garlic, minced
2 cans chicken broth
1-1/4 pounds small red potatoes, halved
1 cup baby carrots
1 cup celery, sliced
1/2 cup small boiling onions
2 teaspoons dried thyme
1 cup portobello mushrooms, halved

Brown chicken in a skillet with garlic and butter. Pour broth in a slow cooker. Add potatoes, carrots, celery, onion, thyme, and mushrooms. Place chicken on top. Cover and cook on low for 7 to 9 hours.

Cowboy Stew

1-1/2 pounds ground beef, browned and drained
pinch of salt and pepper
3 to 4 potatoes, cubed
1 onion, chopped
1 can ranch-style beans

Place all ingredients in a slow cooker. Cook on low for 4 to 6 hours or on high for 1-1/2 to 2 hours. Makes 4 servings.

Vegetable and Barley Soup

2 tablespoons garlic, minced
1/2 cup red onion, chopped
1/2 cup yellow onion, chopped
6 tablespoons sun-dried tomatoes (not marinated), chopped
1 cup red bell pepper, chopped
2 tablespoons olive oil
2 cups button mushrooms, sliced
1/2 cup fresh shiitake mushrooms, sliced
2 tablespoons dried porcini or black-trumpet mushrooms, crumbled
8 cups water
1/4 cup beef broth
1 cup tomatoes, diced
1 cup celery, sliced
1-1/4 cups carrots, sliced
1/2 cup green beans, quartered
1/2 cup yellow squash, sliced
1/2 cup zucchini, sliced
2 tablespoons Dijon mustard
3 bay leaves
3/4 teaspoon ground white pepper, or more to taste
1/2 teaspoon kosher salt, or more to taste
1/2 cup tomato paste
1-1/2 teaspoons dried thyme
3/8 teaspoon dried dill
1-1/8 teaspoons dried oregano
1/4 cup barley
2 tablespoons dried lentils
1/4 cup parsley, chopped
1/4 cup fresh basil, chopped

Place all ingredients in a slow cooker and cook on high 4 to 6 hours or on low 6 to 8 hours. Remove bay leaves. Add salt and pepper.

Mexican Chicken Soup

2 pounds boneless, skinless chicken breasts, cubed
3 cups chicken stock or broth
1 (15-ounce) can black soy beans
1 cup tomatoes, chopped
1 cup scallions, chopped and divided
1/4 cup jalapeños, chopped
2 garlic cloves, crushed
1/2 teaspoon cumin
1/2 teaspoon Mexican oregano
2 tablespoons lime juice
1 cup cheddar cheese, shredded
1/2 cup sour cream

Mix the chicken, broth, soy beans, tomatoes, 3/4 cup scallions (including all of the white parts), jalapeños, garlic, cumin, and oregano in a slow cooker. Cover and cook on high for 1 hour and then on low for at least 5 hours. Add the lime juice and mix well. Place in individual bowls and top evenly with the cheese, sour cream, and reserved green scallions. Makes 6 servings.

THICK AND SPICY CHILI

3 cans chili beans
1 (8-ounce) can tomato sauce
1 (6-ounce) can tomato paste
1/2 teaspoon red pepper
1-1/2 pounds ground beef
1 small onion, chopped
1 (8-ounce) can sliced mushrooms
1 teaspoon chili powder
1 teaspoon garlic powder
1 teaspoon seasoning salt
1/8 cup sugar

Put all of the ingredients in a slow cooker. Cover and cook on low for 8 to 10 hours or on high for 4 to 6 hours.

WHITE BEAN CHILI

1 small onion, chopped
1 tablespoon butter
1 (15-ounce) can great Northern beans
1 (5-ounce) can chunk-style turkey
1/2 cup chicken broth
1/4 cup green chili peppers, chopped
1/2 teaspoon chili powder
1/4 teaspoon garlic powder
1/2 cup Monterey Jack cheese, shredded

Place all ingredients except cheese in a slow cooker. Stir to mix. Cover and cook on low for 6 to 8 hours. Top with cheese.

DUTCH COUNTRY SOUP

1/2 pound frankfurters, cut into 1-inch pieces
1/2 cup onion, chopped
1/4 teaspoon thyme leaves, crushed
2 tablespoons butter or margarine
1 can split pea with ham soup, undiluted
1 cup water
1/2 cup chicken broth
1 can diced carrots, drained
dash of pepper

Place all ingredients in a slow cooker in the order listed. Cover and cook on low for 4 to 6 hours. Makes 4 servings.

Brown Rice and Mushroom Soup

3/4 cup long grain brown rice
1/2 pound mushrooms, finely chopped
1 onion, finely chopped
1 celery stalk, finely chopped
1 teaspoon ground mustard
1 teaspoon fresh ground pepper
1/2 teaspoon salt
1/4 teaspoon ground coriander
1/8 teaspoon ground cardamom
1/8 teaspoon ground cinnamon
1/8 teaspoon ground cloves
4-1/4 cups vegetable or chicken stock
1/3 cup fresh cilantro, chopped
1/2 cup nonfat plain yogurt or sour cream
3 tablespoons scallions, finely chopped

Combine the first twelve ingredients in a slow cooker. Cover and cook on low 5 to 6 hours, or until rice is tender. Stir in cilantro. Serve topped with a dollop of yogurt and sprinkled with scallions.

MOROCCAN LENTIL STEW

1 cup dried lentils, sorted and rinsed
1 pound butternut squash, peeled and cubed
10 small new red potatoes, cubed
1 onion, chopped
4 garlic cloves, minced
2 (14-ounce) cans diced tomatoes, undrained
1 tablespoon curry powder
1/2 teaspoon salt
1/8 teaspoon white pepper
1/8 teaspoon crushed red pepper
2 cups water
1 (8–ounce) package frozen cut green beans, thawed

Combine all ingredients except green beans in a slow cooker. Cover
and cook on low for 8 to 10 hours until lentils, squash, and potatoes
are tender when tested with knife. Increase heat to high setting. Stir in
thawed green beans, cover, and cook for 10 to 15 minutes until
mixture is thoroughly heated and beans are tender. Makes 6 servings.

CRAB STEW

2 cups imitation crab meat, flaked and picked
2 cups milk, whole
2 cups half-and-half
3 tablespoons butter, unsalted
2 lemon peel strips
1/2 teaspoon mace, ground
salt and pepper, to taste
1/2 cup saltine crackers, crushed

Combine all ingredients except crushed crackers in a slow cooker; stir well. Cover and cook on low for 3 to 5 hours. Just before serving, stir in cracker crumbs to thicken.

RAVIOLI STEW

2 cups carrots, sliced
1 onion, chopped
2 garlic cloves, minced
2 (14-ounce) cans vegetable broth
2 (14-ounce) cans Italian style diced tomatoes, undrained
1 (18-ounce) can cannellini beans, rinsed and drained
1 teaspoon dried basil leaves
1/8 teaspoon pepper
1 (9-ounce) package refrigerated cheese stuffed ravioli
1/2 cup Parmesan cheese, grated

Combine all ingredients except ravioli and Parmesan cheese in a slow cooker. Cover slow cooker and cook on low for 6 hours until carrots are tender. Increase heat to high and stir in ravioli. Cover slow cooker and cook for 6 to 8 minutes until ravioli are tender. Sprinkle with cheese and serve. Makes 4 servings.

BLACK-EYED PEA SOUP

2 cups dried black-eyed peas, sorted, rinsed and drained
1 pound smoked turkey sausage, cubed
4 carrots, chopped
1/2 cup wheat berries
1 cup water
3 (14-ounce) cans beef broth

Cover peas with cold water and bring to a boil. Cover and let stand for 1 hour. Drain peas and rinse. Combine all ingredients in a slow cooker, cover, and cook on low for 8 to 9 hours, until peas and wheat berries are tender.

MEATBALL SOUP

1 (16-ounce) bag frozen, fully cooked meatballs
2 (14-ounce) cans condensed beef broth
1 cup water
2 (14-ounce) cans diced tomatoes with herbs, undrained
1 (16-ounce) bag frozen mixed vegetables

Combine frozen meatballs, broth, water, and tomatoes in a slow cooker. Cover and cook on low for 9 to 10 hours, or until meatballs are tender when pierced with a fork. Stir in the frozen vegetables and mix well. Cover and cook on high for 1 hour.

TEX-MEX BEEF STEW

1 pound beef chuck pot roast
1 tablespoon olive oil
2 (14-ounce) cans Mexican diced tomatoes, undrained
2 onions, chopped
3 garlic cloves, minced
2 (15-ounce) cans pinto beans, rinsed and drained
3 cups beef broth
1 (6-ounce) can tomato paste
1 (4-ounce) can chopped jalapeño peppers, undrained
1 tablespoon chili powder
1/4 teaspoon crushed red pepper flakes
1/4 teaspoon ground cloves
1/4 teaspoon ground cinnamon
1/2 teaspoon salt
1/8 teaspoon pepper
1 zucchini, chopped
2 yellow bell peppers, chopped

Cut meat into 1-inch pieces and trim excess fat. Sauté meat in the olive oil over medium heat in a non-stick skillet until browned, about 5 to 6 minutes. Drain well. Place in a slow cooker. Add remaining ingredients except zucchini and yellow bell peppers. Cover and cook on low for 10 to 12 hours until beef is cooked and vegetables are tender.

Turn heat to high, add zucchini and peppers. Cover and cook for 20 to 30 minutes until thoroughly heated. Makes 6 to 8 servings.

Sweet and Sour Chicken Stew

1 pound boneless, skinless chicken breasts, cut into 1-inch pieces
1 (9-ounce) package baby carrots
1 onion, chopped
1 (14-ounce) can condensed chicken broth
1-1/2 cups water
1 tablespoon ginger root, finely chopped
1 (10-ounce) jar sweet and sour simmer sauce
1 (8-ounce) can pineapple chunks, drained, juice reserved
2 tablespoons cornstarch
1 red bell pepper, chopped
1 yellow bell pepper, chopped
1 cup thin egg noodles

Combine chicken, carrots, onion, chicken broth, water, ginger root, and sweet and sour sauce in a slow cooker. Cover and cook on low for 7 to 8 hours, until vegetables are tender and chicken is thoroughly cooked.

Mix reserved pineapple juice with cornstarch until smooth and stir into chicken mixture in a slow cooker, mixing well. Stir in pineapple, bell peppers, and egg noodles. Cover and cook on high for 25 to 35 minutes, or until pasta is tender and vegetables are heated through. Makes 6 to 8 servings.

DOUBLE CORN STEW

3 cups frozen corn
1 (14-ounce) can creamed corn
1 onion, chopped
1 (14-ounce) can chicken broth
1/8 teaspoon pepper

Combine all ingredients in a slow cooker and stir gently to mix.
Cover and cook on low for 5 to 6 hours or until corn is tender.

VEGETABLE MINESTRONE

4 cups vegetable broth or stock
4 cups tomato juice
1 tablespoon dried basil
1 teaspoon salt
1/2 teaspoon dried basil leaves
1/8 teaspoon pepper
2 carrots, sliced
2 celery stalks, chopped
1 onion, chopped
2 garlic cloves, minced
1 cup mushrooms, sliced
2 (14-ounce) cans diced tomatoes, undrained
1-1/2 cups uncooked rotini pasta
Parmesan cheese, grated

Mix all ingredients except pasta and cheese in a slow cooker. Cover
and cook on low for 7 to 8 hours, until vegetables are tender. Stir in
pasta. Cover and cook on high setting for 15 to 25 minutes until pasta
is tender. Sprinkle each serving with freshly Parmesan cheese, grated.
Makes 12 servings.

RUSTIC CHICKEN STEW

**2 pounds boneless, skinless chicken breasts, washed, patted dry,
cut into 1-inch cubes**
3 medium onions, peeled and quartered
2 large carrots, peeled, cut into 1-inch-thick slices
2 potatoes, peeled, cut into 1-inch cubes
2 (14-ounce) cans fat-free, 1/3-less-sodium chicken broth
1 teaspoon celery seed
1 teaspoon dried thyme leaves
1/2 teaspoon black pepper
1 cup mushrooms, cleaned and halved
1 cup frozen corn
1 cup frozen peas

In a slow cooker, combine the chicken, onions, carrots, potatoes, and broth. Stir in the celery seeds, thyme, pepper, mushrooms, and corn.

Cover and cook on low until the chicken is done and the vegetables are tender, about 7 to 9 hours, or on high for 4 to 6 hours. Stir in the peas and cook until they're done, about 15 to 30 minutes.

VEGETARIAN CHILI

2 large onions, diced
2 tablespoons olive oil
3 garlic cloves, minced
2 teaspoons cumin
1 tablespoon chili powder
1 red bell pepper, chopped
1 green bell pepper, chopped
3 (14-ounce) cans diced tomatoes, undrained
1/2 teaspoon crushed red pepper flakes
1 (10-ounce) package frozen corn
2 (15-ounce) cans black beans, drained and rinsed
1 cup picante sauce

In a heavy skillet, sauté onions in the olive oil until tender, stirring
frequently. Add garlic and cook 2 minutes longer. Add cumin and
chili powder. Cook for 2 minutes longer. Mix all ingredients into a
slow cooker. Cover and cook on low about 10 hours. Makes 8 to 10
servings.

Yellow Pea Chowder

1 pound package dried yellow split peas, sorted and rinsed
4 cups water
1 (10-ounce) can condensed chicken broth
1 cup smoked chorizo sausage, sliced
1/4 teaspoon salt
1/8 teaspoon pepper
1 cup carrot, chopped
1 (11-ounce) can corn with red and green peppers, drained

Combine all ingredients except corn in a slow cooker and stir to mix. Cover and cook on low for 7 to 9 hours. Stir in corn about 10 minutes before serving. Increase heat to high, cover, and cook 10 minutes longer.

VEGETABLE AND BEEF SOUP

1 cup frozen green beans
1 cup frozen corn
1-1/2 pounds beef stew meat
1 green bell pepper, chopped
1 onion, chopped
2 garlic cloves, minced
2/3 cup uncooked pearl barley
1-1/2 cups water
1/2 teaspoon salt
1/2 teaspoon dried thyme leaves
1/4 teaspoon pepper
2 (14-ounce) cans ready to serve beef broth
2 (14-ounce) cans diced tomatoes with roasted garlic, undrained
1 (8-ounce) can tomato sauce

Mix all ingredients in a slow cooker. Cover and cook on low heat for 8 to 9 hours, or high setting for 4 to 5 hours, until vegetables, stew meat, and barley are tender, stirring once during cooking time.

CURRY CAULIFLOWER SOUP

1 pound cauliflower florets, cooked
1-3/4 pounds canned diced tomatoes, undrained
1 (14-ounce) vegetable or beef stock
1 onion, chopped and cooked
1/2 teaspoon garlic powder
2 teaspoon curry powder
1/8 teaspoon ground cumin

Combine all ingredients in a slow cooker on low heat. Cover and cook about 7 hours, or until cauliflower is tender. Increase heat to high. Add salt and pepper to taste. Cover and cook another 30 minutes. Serve hot or cold.

Chicken Chili

2 pounds boneless, skinless chicken thighs
3 (14-ounce) cans diced tomatoes with chilies and garlic,
  undrained
1 (1-ounce) package taco seasoning mix
2 (15-ounce) cans white beans, drained and rinsed

Combine all ingredients in a slow cooker. Cover and cook on low for 7 to 9 hours, or until chicken is tender. Stir well so the chicken breaks into small pieces.

Mexican Beef Soup

1 pound beef stew meat, cut into 1/2-inch cubes
1 (14-ounce) can beef stock
2 cups water
1 pound Mexican style frozen vegetables
1 (14-ounce) can Mexican style chunky tomato sauce
1 pound canned pinto beans, rinsed and drained
2 teaspoons ground cumin
1 pound canned black beans, rinsed and drained
1/4 teaspoon seasoned salt
1/4 teaspoon garlic pepper
1/2 cup sour cream

Combine first seven ingredients in a slow cooker on low heat. Cover and cook 8 to 8-1/2 hours, or until beef is tender. Increase heat to high. Stir in remaining ingredients, except sour cream. Cover and heat another 10 to 20 minutes, until hot. Serve with a dollop of sour cream.

KIELBASA STEW

1-1/2 pounds low fat turkey kielbasa, cut into 1-inch pieces
2 pounds sauerkraut, rinsed and drained
3 Granny Smith apples, peeled, cored, and cut into rings
1 onion, cooked and thinly sliced
2-1/4 pounds red potatoes, quartered
2 cups chicken stock
1/2 teaspoon caraway seeds
1/2 cup fat-free Swiss cheese, grated

Place half the sausage in a slow cooker and top with sauerkraut.
Cover with remaining sausage, apple, and onion. Top with potatoes.
Add stock and sprinkle with caraway seeds. Cover and cook on high
for 4 hours, or until potatoes are tender. Serve sprinkled with cheese.

BEAN SOUP

2-1/4 pounds mixed dried beans
2 onions, chopped
10 cups water
1 teaspoon dried thyme leaves
4 carrots, chopped
1 (14-ounce) can diced tomatoes, undrained

Combine all ingredients in a slow cooker except for tomatoes and stir
well to combine. Cover and cook on high for 8 to 10 hours or until
beans are tender. Add tomatoes, stir, cover, and cook on high for 15 to
20 minutes longer until heated. Makes 12 servings.

POTATO-CHEESE SOUP

8 potatoes, cubed
1 tablespoon chives, chopped
1-1/2 cups celery, chopped
1/3 cup parsley, chopped
1/2 cup onion, chopped
1/4 teaspoon paprika
1/4 teaspoon celery seed
1 teaspoon savory
1/2 teaspoon salt
1 cup milk
2 tablespoons flour
2 tablespoons butter
2-1/2 cups cheddar cheese, grated

Combine potatoes, chives, celery, parsley, onion, paprika, celery seed, savory, and salt in a slow cooker; add water to cover. Cook on high for 1 hour. Turn heat to low and cook 4 to 5 hours or until potatoes are done. Combine milk and flour thoroughly. In a small saucepan, melt butter over medium heat. Add flour mixture slowly, and stir constantly 3 to 4 minutes. Add cheese; stir until melted. Turn slow cooker to high setting. Add cheese mixture to soup and cook until slightly thickened.

MOROCCAN SOUP

**2 pounds turkey breast or thighs, cut in 1/2-pound chunks and
  skin removed
1-1/2 cups lentils, rinsed
1 cup onion, chopped
1 cup celery, chopped
2 tablespoons tomato paste
1 teaspoon ground turmeric
1/2 teaspoon ground cinnamon
7 cups turkey broth
2 tablespoons fresh lemon juice
salt and pepper, to taste**

Place thighs or breasts in a slow cooker. Add lentils, onion, celery,
tomato paste, turmeric, cinnamon, and turkey broth; stir well. Cover
and set temperature to high or low. Cook soup until turkey is tender, 3
to 5 hours on high or 7 to 9 hours on low. Transfer turkey from soup
to cutting board and cut into bite-sized pieces; return to soup. Discard
bones. Heat mixture to 160°. Season to taste with lemon juice, salt,
and pepper.

This recipe used by permission of the National Turkey Federation.

CHINESE TURKEY STEW

1 pound boneless, skinless turkey thighs, cut into 1-inch cubes
1 teaspoon Chinese 5-spice powder
1/2 teaspoon red pepper flakes
1 tablespoon peanut oil
1 large sweet onion, coarsely chopped
8 ounces button mushrooms, cleaned and sliced
2 garlic cloves, minced
14 ounces turkey broth
1 tablespoon cornstarch
1 large red bell pepper, seeded and cut into cubes
2 tablespoons soy sauce
1 tablespoon sesame oil
1/3 cup green onions, chopped
1/4 cup fresh cilantro

Toss turkey cubes with 5-spice powder and red pepper flakes in a small bowl. Heat oil in a large skillet over medium heat. Sauté turkey and onion in oil until turkey is brown and onions are soft.

Stir in mushrooms and continue to cook until turkey is no longer pink. Add garlic and cook for 30 seconds. Remove from heat.

In a small bowl, combine 1⁄4 cup turkey broth with cornstarch. Cover and refrigerate.

Place turkey mixture, remaining broth, red pepper cubes and soy sauce in slow cooker. Stir well. Cover and cook on low for 3-1⁄2 hours or until peppers are soft. Add cornstarch mixture, sesame oil, and green onions, stirring well. Cook an additional 30 to 45, minutes or until juices become thickened. Portion into soup bowls and garnish with cilantro.

This recipe used by permission of the National Turkey Federation.

Turkey Chili and Beans

1 pound ground turkey
2 (14-ounce) cans whole peeled tomatoes, drained
2 (14-ounce) cans kidney beans, drained and rinsed
1 (14-ounce) can black beans, drained and rinsed
1 (12-ounce) can tomato sauce
1 cup celery, finely chopped
1 cup carrot, finely chopped
1 cup onion, finely chopped
3 tablespoons chili powder
4 teaspoons ground cumin
2 teaspoons ground red pepper
1 teaspoon salt
1/2 cup water
1/2 cup Monterey Jack cheese, shredded

Cook ground turkey in a heavy skillet over medium heat until the pink color disappears. Place cooked ground turkey and all other ingredients, except cheese, in a slow cooker. Mix well and cook on high for 7 hours. Garnish with cheese.

For a thicker sauce, remove the cover for the last hour.

This recipe used by permission of the National Turkey Federation.

WHITE TURKEY CHILI

1 cup onion, chopped
1 cup celery, chopped
4 cups turkey, cooked and chopped
2 (15-1/2-ounce) cans great Northern beans, drained
2 (11-ounce) cans white shoepeg corn, undrained
1 (4-ounce) can chopped green chilies
1 quart turkey broth
1 teaspoon ground cumin
1/2 cup Mozzarella cheese, grated

Place cooked turkey and all other ingredients in a slow cooker. Mix well and cook on low for 6 to 8 hours. Sprinkle with Mozzarella cheese.

For a thicker sauce, remove the cover for the last hour.

This recipe used by permission of the National Turkey Federation.

PORK AND BLACK BEAN STEW

1-1/2 pounds pork, cut in 1-inch pieces
1/2 cup flour
1 teaspoon chili powder
1/2 teaspoon salt
1/4 teaspoon ground black pepper
2 tablespoons olive oil
1-1/2 cups onion, chopped
1/2 pound pork sausage
1 (10-1/2-ounce) can condensed chicken broth
1/4 cup parsley, chopped
3 large garlic cloves, minced
1 (4-ounce) small can chopped mild green chile peppers, optional
dash of oregano
2 (15-ounce) cans black beans, drained and rinsed
1 cup frozen corn kernels
1 large red bell pepper, chopped
2 plum tomatoes, diced
1 teaspoon lemon juice
salt and pepper, to taste
diced tomato and green onion, for garnish (optional)

Toss pork in a food storage bag with flour, chili powder, 1/2 teaspoon salt, and 1/4 teaspoon black pepper. Heat olive oil in a large skillet. Add coated pork to the skillet along with any remaining flour; brown on all sides. Pour into a slow cooker. Add pork sausage and onions to skillet and brown lightly; add to slow cooker. Add the condensed chicken broth, parsley, and garlic. Cook on low for 9 to 11 hours, or on high for 4-1/2 to 6 hours.

About 2 hours before done (or 1 hour if cooking on high), add the chili peppers, oregano, black beans, corn, bell pepper, diced plum tomatoes, and lemon juice.

Taste and adjust seasoning. Serve in bowls, with cornbread and a garnish of diced tomatoes and green onions. Makes 6 to 8 servings.

VEGETABLES
AND
SIDE DISHES

VEGETARIAN STUFFED PEPPERS

2 large green bell peppers
2 large red bell peppers
1/2 cup converted white rice
1 (15-ounce) can whole kernel corn, drained
1 (2-ounce) can sliced ripe olives, drained
3 green onions, chopped
1/4 teaspoon seasoned salt
1/4 teaspoon garlic pepper
1 (14-1/2-ounce) can diced tomatoes, undrained, divided
1/3 cup vegetable broth
1 (6-ounce) can tomato paste

Slice tops off peppers and carefully remove seeds and inner ribs.
Remove stems from tops and chop remaining pepper pieces. Stand
the peppers upright in a slow cooker. In a medium bowl, combine
chopped pepper tops, rice, corn, olives, green onions, seasoned salt,
garlic pepper, and 1/4 cup tomatoes. Mix well. Stuff peppers with
corn mixture, dividing evenly and packing lightly. Mix remaining
tomatoes and their liquid with broth and tomato paste until well
blended. Pour over and around the peppers in slow cooker. Cover and
cook on low for 6 to 7 hours, or until rice is cooked and peppers are
tender, but still hold their shape.

SLOW COOKER CARAMELIZED ONIONS

6 large onions
2 tablespoons olive oil

Peel the onions and cut them into 1/4-inch slices. Place the onions in
the slow cooker and sprinkle with oil. Cover and cook 8 to 10 hours,
until the onions caramelize. Makes 3 cups.

SOUTHERN POTATOES

2 pounds frozen hash browns
1 (10-1/2-ounce) can cream of mushroom soup
1/2 cup butter, melted
2 cups French onion dip

Mix together all ingredients and put into a slow cooker. Cook on low for 6 to 8 hours. Add French onion dip 30 minutes before serving.

BAKED BEANS

1/2 pound ground beef, cooked and drained
1 small onion, chopped
1/4 cup brown sugar
1/4 cup ketchup
1/4 cup barbecue sauce
2 tablespoons prepared mustard
2 tablespoons molasses
1/2 teaspoon chili powder
1 teaspoon salt
1/4 teaspoon pepper
1 can red kidney beans, drained
1 can butter beans, drained
1 can pork and beans

Combine all ingredients in a slow cooker. Cover and cook on low for 6 to 8 hours.

GINGERED CARROTS

12 carrots, peeled and sliced
1/3 cup Dijon mustard
1/2 cup brown sugar
1 teaspoon ginger, minced
1/8 teaspoon pepper
1/2 teaspoon salt

Combine all ingredients in a slow cooker. Cover and cook on high for 2 to 3 hours or until carrots are tender, stirring twice during cooking.

SALT BAKED POTATOES

baking potatoes
bacon fat or cooking oil
large bag of kosher salt

Scrub potatoes well, then dry thoroughly with paper towels, prick with fork, and rub with bacon fat or cooking oil. Put about an inch depth of salt into a slow cooker, lay potatoes on salt, and pour remainder of bag of salt over top so the potatoes are evenly covered. Cover slow cooker and cook on high for about 2 hours, until potatoes are tender when tested with a fork (you can stick a fork through the salt to test doneness). Turn off slow cooker and potatoes will keep warm until you are ready to serve. Break through the salt crust and lift out the potatoes, brushing gently to remove any salt.

HOME-STYLE BAKED BEANS

2-1/2 cups dry beans
1 small onion, chopped
1/2 teaspoon pepper
1/4 cup brown sugar
1-1/2 teaspoons salt
6 tablespoons ketchup
6 tablespoons molasses
1 (2-ounce) piece of salt pork
1 tablespoon dry mustard

Soak beans overnight in water. The next day, boil beans for 1 hour. Add salt pork, onions, and all other ingredients. Cook in a slow cooker on high for 3 hours, or low for 10 to 12 hours. Add water as needed.

HOTDOG BEANS

1-1/2 tablespoons yellow mustard
1/3 cup ketchup (for spicier beans, use barbecue sauce)
1/4 cup dark brown sugar
1/2 teaspoon onion powder
2 (16-ounce) cans of baked beans (dark brown, small beans work best)
1 package hot dogs, sliced

Mix all ingredients together in a slow cooker. Cook for 1-1/2 to 2-1/2 hours on high or 4 to 8 hours on low.

GLAZED CARROTS

2 pounds baby carrots
1-1/2 cups water
1/4 cup honey
2 tablespoons butter
1/4 teaspoon salt
1/8 teaspoon pepper

Combine carrots and water in a slow cooker. Cover and cook on low for 6 to 8 hours, or until carrots are tender when pierced with a fork. Drain carrots and return to slow cooker. Stir in honey, butter, salt, and pepper and mix well. Cover and cook on low 30 minutes until glazed.

MAGNIFICENT MUSHROOMS

1 pound mushrooms, sliced or whole
1/2 cup butter
1 tablespoon marjoram
1 teaspoon chives, minced
salt and pepper, to taste
3/4 cup chicken broth

Place mushrooms in a slow cooker. Place butter on top. Mix remaining ingredients and pour over the top. Cover and cook on low for 4 to 6 hours.

PEACHY SWEET POTATOES

2 pounds dark orange sweet potatoes
1 cup peach pie filling
2 tablespoons butter, melted
1/4 teaspoon salt
1/4 teaspoon pepper

Spray a slow cooker with non-stick cooking spray and place sweet potatoes in the slow cooker. Add pie filling, melted butter, salt, and pepper and mix well. Cover and cook on high for 2-1/2 to 3-1/2 hours until potatoes are tender when pierced with a fork.

RICE PILAF

2 (14-ounce) cans chicken broth with roasted garlic
1-2/3 cups water
3 cups converted long grain white rice
1/2 cup onion, minced
1/4 teaspoon pepper

Combine broth and water in a large bowl and microwave on high until very hot, about 5 minutes. Spray a slow cooker with cooking spray. Combine rice, onion, and pepper in slow cooker and mix to combine. Pour hot broth mixture over and cover slow cooker. Cook on high for 1-1/2 to 2 hours, until rice is tender. Stir and serve.

CHEESY BROCCOLI AND CAULIFLOWER

1 (10-ounce) package frozen broccoli
1 (10-ounce) package frozen cauliflower
salt and pepper, to taste
1 can condensed nacho cheese soup
4 slices bacon, cooked and crumbled

Place broccoli and cauliflower in a slow cooker. Season with salt and pepper to taste. Spoon soup over top. Sprinkle with bacon. Cover and cook on low for 4 to 6 hours. Makes 4 to 6 servings.

MASHED POTATOES

5 pounds potatoes, peeled and quartered
1 (8-ounce) package light cream cheese
1 cup light sour cream
2 teaspoons onion powder
1 teaspoon salt
1/2 teaspoon black pepper
2 egg whites, slightly beaten
1 tablespoon margarine

Cook the potatoes in a large pot of boiling water until they are tender, about 20 minutes. Drain; mash until there are no lumps. Add the cream cheese, sour cream, onion powder, salt, pepper, and egg whites; blend well. Spray a casserole with non-stick cooking spray. Add potato mixture. Dot with margarine. Cool slightly, cover, and refrigerate up to 7 days. Take potatoes out of refrigerator about 3-1/2 hours before you plan to serve them. Place in a slow cooker. Dot with margarine or butter. Cook on low heat for 3 hours, stirring once or twice. They can be held an additional 30 minutes or more.

Hot German Potato Salad

6 cups raw potato, sliced
1 cup onion, chopped
1 cup celery, chopped
1/2 cup water
1/4 cup cider vinegar
1 tablespoon sugar
2 tablespoons quick cooking tapioca
1/4 teaspoon black pepper
2 teaspoons dried parsley flakes
1/4 cup bacon bits

In a large bowl, combine potatoes, onion, and celery. Mix remaining ingredients except bacon in a small bowl; pour over potatoes, mixing well. Pour into slow cooker. Cover and cook on low for 8 to 10 hours, until potatoes are done. Stir in bacon bits.

Macaroni and Cheese

1 (16-ounce) box of macaroni
1/2 cup margarine
2 (12-ounce) cans evaporated milk
3 cups milk
3 cups sharp cheese, grated
1 tablespoon onion, minced (optional)
1 tablespoon oil
1 teaspoon salt
pepper, to taste

Put all the ingredients into a slow cooker. Cook on low for 3 to 4 hours until soft.

WILD RICE

1-1/2 cups regular long grain rice
1/2 cup wild rice
1 envelope onion soup mix
1 tablespoon parsley (dried is fine)
4 cups water
1 bunch green onions, sliced
1 (8-ounce) can mushrooms, sliced (fresh is better)

Combine all ingredients into a lightly greased slow cooker. Cook 2 to 2-1/2 hours on high. Stir occasionally, especially near end of cooking.

CHEESY SPINACH

2 (10-ounce) packages frozen chopped spinach, thawed and well
  drained
2 cups small-curd cottage cheese
1-1/2 cups cheese (cheddar or processed American cheese)
3 eggs, lightly beaten
1/4 cup margarine, cubed
1/4 cup flour
1 teaspoon salt

Combine all the ingredients in a large bowl. Pour into a greased slow cooker. Cover and cook on high for 1 hour. Reduce heat to low and cook 4 to 5 hours longer, or until a knife inserted comes out clean. Makes 6 to 8 servings.

FRESH VEGGIE LASAGNA

1-1/2 cups Mozzarella cheese, shredded
1/2 cup part-skim ricotta cheese
1/3 cup Parmesan cheese, grated
1 egg, lightly beaten
1 teaspoon dried oregano
1/4 teaspoon garlic powder
1 cup low-sodium, fat-free marinara sauce (plus additional for
  serving)
1 medium zucchini, diced
4 no-boil lasagna noodles
1 bag baby spinach
1 cup mushrooms, thinly sliced
fresh basil leaves (optional)

Spray crock pot of a slow cooker with non-stick cooking spray; set aside. In a small bowl, mix together mozzarella, ricotta, Parmesan, egg, oregano, and garlic powder.

Spread 2 tablespoons of marinara sauce in bottom of pot. Sprinkle half of the zucchini over sauce and top with one-third of cheese mixture. Break two noodles into pieces to cover cheese. Spread 2 tablespoons of sauce and then layer half of the spinach and half of the mushrooms. Repeat layering, ending with cheese and remaining sauce. Firmly press ingredients into pot.

Cover and cook over low heat for 4 to 5 hours. Allow lasagna to rest 20 minutes before cutting into wedges to serve. Spoon a little extra sauce over each serving and top with a basil leaf, if desired.

HARVEST POTATOES

1 cup chicken broth
2 teaspoons pickling spice, tied in cheesecloth
4 large potatoes, peeled and cut into 3/4-inch cubes
2 garlic cloves, pressed
snipped fresh chives, for garnish (optional)

Pour the broth into a slow cooker, and place the spices in the center bottom of the cooker. Add the potatoes and garlic. Cover and cook on low for 5 to 6 hours. Garnish with chives.

CINNAMON APPLESAUCE

10 large apples, peeled, cored, and chopped
1/2 cup water
1 teaspoon cinnamon
1/2 teaspoon nutmeg
1 cup sugar

Put all ingredients into a slow cooker. Cover and cook on low for 8 to 10 hours.

CHEESY POTATOES

1 (10-ounce) can condensed cream of mushroom soup
1 (8-ounce) container sour cream
1-1/2 cups cheddar cheese, shredded
1 (32-ounce) package frozen hash brown potatoes

Spray slow cooker with cooking spray. Combine soup, sour cream, and cheese in medium bowl; mix well. Pour half of potatoes into a prepared slow cooker. Top with half of the sour cream mixture. Top with rest of potatoes, then remaining sour cream mixture, spreading evenly. Cover and cook on high for 3-1/2 to 4-1/2 hours.

BARBECUE PINTO BEANS

1 pound dried pinto beans
3 cups water
1 onion, chopped
1 (18-ounce) bottle barbecue sauce
1/4 cup molasses
1/4 teaspoon pepper

Sort beans, rinse, and drain. Combine all ingredients in a slow cooker. Cover and cook on low for 8 to 9 hours, or until beans are tender. Makes 6 to 8 servings.

MIXED RICE PILAF

3/4 cup wild rice
1/2 cup long grain brown rice
1/2 pound portobello mushrooms
1 (10-ounce) can cream of mushroom soup with roasted garlic
1-1/2 cups water
1/8 teaspoon pepper

Rinse rice and drain. Wipe mushrooms with a damp cloth, remove stems, and cut into 1-inch slices. Combine all ingredients in a slow cooker. Cover and cook on low for 6 to 7 hours or until rice and mushrooms are tender.

VEGETARIAN ENCHILADA CASSEROLE

3-1/3 cups canned crushed tomatoes
1-2/3 cups chunky style prepared salsa
1 (6-ounce) can tomato paste
2 pounds canned black beans, rinsed and drained
1 pound corn kernels, thawed if frozen
1/4 pound canned diced mild green chilies, drained
1-1/2 tablespoons ground cumin
1/2 teaspoon garlic powder
6 corn tortillas
1/4 cup olive slices, drained

Combine first eight ingredients in a bowl. Mix thoroughly. Pour about 1 cup of mixture into the bottom of a slow cooker on low heat. Spread evenly and top with 3 tortillas, cutting to fit pot. Spread 1/3 of remaining tomato mixture over top. Repeat layering process, ending with tomato mixture. Spread top evenly. Sprinkle with olives. Cover and cook about 5 hours. Serve hot.

BEEF, PORK, AND LAMB

BEEF AND BROCCOLI

3/4 pounds thin beef strips
2 cups fresh broccoli flowerets
1 package McCormick Brown Gravy Mix
1 cup water

Place beef and broccoli in the bottom of a slow cooker. Mix together gravy mix and water. Pour over the top. Cover and cook on low for 6 to 8 hours.

VIENNESE POT ROAST

1 onion, chopped
2 carrots, chopped
2 turnips, chopped
8 new potatoes
4 dried figs, chopped
3/4 cup chicken stock
3/4 cup beef stock
1 (4-pound) rump roast
4 gingersnap cookies, crushed

Place vegetables in the bottom of a slow cooker. Add the figs, chicken, and beef stock. Add the roast on top. Cover and cook on low for 8 to 10 hours. Set to high heat and add gingersnap cookies; cook until thickened.

Teriyaki Steak

2 tablespoons vegetable oil
1 teaspoon ground ginger
1/2 cup soy sauce
1 tablespoon sugar
1 garlic clove, crushed
2-1/2 pounds boneless chuck steak, cut into thin slices

Combine all ingredients except steak. Place meat in a slow cooker. Pour sauce on top of steak. Cook on low for 6 to 8 hours. Serve over hot rice.

Spiced Beef Brisket

1 (4 to 5-pound) fresh beef brisket
2 cups water
1 (1-ounce) package onion soup mix
1/4 cup ketchup
2 tablespoons Worcestershire sauce
1/2 teaspoon garlic, minced
4 tablespoons flour

Place brisket in a slow cooker. Combine water with soup mix, ketchup, Worcestershire sauce, and garlic. Pour over brisket. Cover and cook on low for 8 to 10 hours.

To make gravy, combine 1/4 cup cold water and 4 tablespoons flour in a small saucepan. Stir until flour dissolves. Add 3/4 cup cooking liquid. Cook and stir until bubbly. Continue cooking for an additional minute. Makes 8 to 12 servings.

HUNGRY MAN SLOW COOKER

1 pound ground beef
1 (16-ounce) can baked beans
3/4 cup barbecue sauce
2/3 cup cheddar cheese, shredded

Brown ground beef and drain. Mix ground beef, baked beans, and barbecue sauce together and put in slow cooker. Cover and cook on low for 6 to 8 hours. Sprinkle with cheddar cheese the last 15 minutes of cooking.

MEXICAN RIBS

4 pounds beef short ribs
1-1/4 cups beef stock
2-1/2 tablespoons taco seasoning mix

Place ribs in the bottom of a slow cooker. Thoroughly mix beef stock and taco seasoning mix, and pour over the ribs. Cover and cook on low for 6 to 8 hours.

ONION MEATBALLS

3 pounds frozen cooked meatballs
1 package dry onion soup mix
3 garlic cloves, minced
1 (10-ounce) jar beef gravy
3 tablespoons water
1/8 teaspoon pepper

Combine all ingredients in a slow cooker and stir to combine. Cover slow cooker and cook on low for 4 to 5 hours until thoroughly heated.

ACAPULCO FLANK STEAK

1-1/2 to 2 pounds beef flank steak
6 fresh tomatillos
1 (15-ounce) can whole baby corn, drained
1/2 teaspoon salt
1/4 teaspoon ground black pepper
1/4 cup fresh cilantro, chopped
1 small red onion, thinly sliced
1/4 cup beef broth

Trim all visible fat from steak. Place steak in a slow cooker. Remove and discard husk and stem from tomatillos. Chop and add to steak. Top with baby corn, salt, pepper, cilantro, and onion. Pour in broth. Cover and cook on low about 6 hours or until steak is tender. Slice steak crosswise into strips. Spoon vegetables and sauce over sliced steak. Makes 6 to 7 servings.

TENDER SHREDDED BEEF

1 (2 pound) fresh beef brisket
1 tablespoon olive oil
1 (10-ounce) can condensed beef broth
2 garlic cloves, minced
1 onion, chopped, if desired
1/2 teaspoon salt
1/4 teaspoon pepper

Trim excess fat from beef. Heat oil in 10-inch skillet over medium heat. Cook beef for 10 minutes, turning frequently, to brown all sides. Place beef in a slow cooker. Pour remaining ingredients over beef. Cover and cook on low heat setting for 8 to 10 hours, until beef is tender. Remove beef from slow cooker and shred, using two forks. Skim fat from juices in slow cooker, and add beef. Keep on low setting until ready to serve and while serving too.

BEEF AND BLACK-EYED PEAS

1 (16-ounce) package dried black-eyed peas
1 (10-ounce) can condensed bean and bacon soup
3 cups water
4 carrots, peeled and chopped
3 pounds beef chuck roast, cut into 2-inch cubes
1/4 teaspoon pepper

Sort through the black-eyed peas to remove any stones or shriveled peas, then rinse and drain. Combine all ingredients in a slow cooker. Cover and cook on low for 9 to 10 hours or until peas are tender and beef is done.

BEACH BOY POT ROAST

1 beef roast
slivers of garlic
1 jar of pepperoncini peppers

Cut some slits in roast and insert garlic slivers. Place beef in a slow cooker. Dump peppers and all of the juice on top. Cook all day on low, at least 12 hours.

For serving, just slice and serve, or make hoagies. Add pepperoncini peppers.

SAUCY BEEF

2 pounds beef stew meat
2 (10-ounce) cans condensed tomato soup
1 (10-ounce) can condensed cheddar cheese soup

Place meat in the slow cooker; pour the soups over the meat and mix well to combine. Cover slow cooker and cook 8 to 10 hours, until meat is tender. Stir well and serve over hot cooked rice or noodles.

Savory Short Ribs

4 pounds beef short ribs
1/2 teaspoon pepper
1 (12-ounce) jar beef gravy
1 pound frozen bell peppers and onions, thawed and drained

In a slow cooker, place ribs and sprinkle with pepper. Pour gravy over top. Cover slow cooker and cook on low for 9 to 11 hours until beef is tender. Skim fat from surface of liquid in slow cooker and remove ribs. Cover to keep warm. Add bell peppers and onions to slow cooker and cover. Cook on high 15 to 20 minutes until hot. Serve vegetables and sauce over ribs.

Beef and Potatoes

3 to 4 potatoes, thinly sliced
1 teaspoon salt
1/2 teaspoon pepper
2 tablespoons butter, melted
1 pound ground beef, browned
1 medium onion, chopped
1 (10-1/2-ounce) can spaghetti sauce

Put potatoes in the bottom of a slow cooker. Sprinkle with salt and pepper. Add remaining ingredients. Cover and cook on low for 8 to 10 hours.

ALL DAY LONG BEEF

1 yellow onion, sliced
3 carrots, diced
2 celery stalks, diced
1 green bell pepper, chopped
1-1/2 pounds beef roast, cut into serving-size pieces
1/2 teaspoon black pepper
2 garlic cloves, minced
1/2 package onion soup mix
2 teaspoons Worcestershire sauce
1 teaspoon steak sauce
1/2 cup water
1/2 cup tomato juice

Slice onion and separate into rings. Place onion, carrots, celery, and bell pepper into bottom of a slow cooker. Sprinkle the beef pieces with fresh ground black pepper, minced garlic, and the onion soup mix. Place on top of the vegetables. Mix the steak sauce and Worcestershire sauce in a small bowl with about 1/2 cup water and 1/2 cup tomato juice. Pour over the meat. Cover and cook on low for 7 to 9 hours.

SMOKY BARBECUE BRISKET

1 (2 to 3-pound) fresh beef brisket
1 teaspoon chili powder
1/2 teaspoon garlic powder
1/4 teaspoon celery seed
1/8 teaspoon pepper
1/2 cup ketchup
1/2 cup chili sauce
1/4 cup packed brown sugar
2 tablespoons vinegar
2 tablespoons Worcestershire sauce
1-1/2 teaspoons liquid smoke
1/2 teaspoon dry mustard

Trim fat from brisket. If necessary, cut brisket to fit slow cooker.
Combine chili powder, garlic powder, celery seed, and pepper; rub
evenly over meat. Place meat in a slow cooker. Combine ketchup,
chili sauce, brown sugar, vinegar, Worcestershire sauce, liquid smoke,
and dry mustard. Pour over brisket. Cover and cook on low for 8 to
12 hours or on high for 4 to 5 hours. Makes 6 to 8 servings.

Mushroom Smothered Beef

1/2 pound fresh white mushrooms, sliced
1 medium onion, sliced
1 can condensed cream of mushroom soup
1/2 cup beef broth
2 tablespoons Worcestershire sauce, divided
1 (4-ounce) can diced green chilies
2-1/2 pound boneless beef chuck or cross rib roast, sliced into
  1-1/2 to 2-inch cubes
3 tablespoons flour

Combine mushrooms and onion in bottom of a slow cooker. Whisk together undiluted soup with the broth, 1 tablespoon of the Worcestershire sauce, and chilies. Pour half of soup mixture over the mushrooms and onion. Place beef on top of the mushroom mixture. Pour the remaining soup mixture on top. Do not mix. Cover and cook on low for 8 hours. Increase the heat setting to high. Mix remaining Worcestershire sauce with flour and several spoonfuls of the liquid from the slow cooker until smooth. Stir the flour mixture into the sauce in the slow cooker. Cover and cook on high for 30 minutes. Makes 5 to 6 servings.

TANGY RUMP ROAST

1 (3 to 5-pound) rump roast, trimmed
1 package onion soup mix
1 can cranberry sauce, jellied
2 tablespoons butter, softened
2 tablespoons flour

Rinse rump roast and pat dry. Sprinkle onion soup mix in bottom of a slow cooker. Place rump roast in next; spoon cranberry sauce around and over roast. Cover and cook on low 10 to 12 hours. Remove roast from slow cooker and allow to rest while you thicken gravy. Turn slow cooker up on high. Blend softened butter and flour into a paste. Whisk it into the gravy. Cover and cook on high for about 10 minutes, until thick. Slice roast into 1/4-inch thick slices and serve with gravy.

ROULADE STEAK

3 pounds round steaks, thinly sliced
1 teaspoon salt
1 teaspoon pepper
3/4 cup onion, chopped
3/4 cup bacon, chopped
1/4 cup water
flour

Trim fat off steaks. Season with salt and pepper. Mix onion and bacon, and spread over each steak. Roll steaks (as you would for a jelly roll), and tie rolls tightly in several places with a string. Put steaks into a slow cooker. Add water. Cover and cook on low for 8 hours. For gravy, remove meat when done, thicken liquid with a mixture of flour and water, and cook it in pot set at high for 15 minutes.

SLOPPY JOES

2 pounds lean ground beef
1 onion, chopped
1/4 cup water
1/2 teaspoon salt
1/4 teaspoon pepper
1 (12-ounce) bottle chili sauce or ketchup

Cook ground beef in a heavy skillet until brown and crumbly. Drain thoroughly and place in slow cooker. Add remaining ingredients and mix well. Cover slow cooker and cook on low for 4 to 6 hours until onions are tender. Serve on sandwich buns or tortilla chips.

HUNGARIAN GOULASH

1-1/2 pounds stewing beef, cut into 3/4-inch pieces
1/2 cup water
1 (8-ounce) can tomato sauce
2 onions, chopped
1 clove garlic, chopped
1 tablespoon paprika
2 teaspoons salt
2 teaspoons beef bouillon
1/4 teaspoon black pepper, coarsely ground
1 cup sour cream

Place all ingredients except sour cream in the bottom of a slow cooker. Cover and cook for 8 to 12 hours on low. Add sour cream to slow cooker 10 minutes before serving. Serve over noodles. Makes 4 servings.

French Dip Sandwich

1 (1-pound) fresh beef brisket
1 package dry onion soup mix
1 (10-ounce) can condensed beef broth

Combine all ingredients in a slow cooker. Cover and cook on low for 8 to 10 hours, until beef is tender. Skim any fat from liquid in slow cooker. Remove beef and cut across the grain into thin slices. Serve on crusty baguette rolls, and serve the hot broth for dipping.

Tamale Pie

3/4 cup yellow cornmeal
1 cup beef broth
1 pound extra-lean ground beef, browned and drained
1 teaspoon chili powder
1/2 teaspoon ground cumin (optional)
1 (14 to 16-ounce) jar thick and chunky salsa
1 (16-ounce) can whole-kernel corn, drained
1/4 cup ripe olives, sliced
1/2 cup cheddar cheese, shredded

In a large bowl, mix cornmeal and broth; let stand 5 minutes. Stir in beef, chili powder, cumin, salsa, corn, and olives. Pour into a slow cooker. Cover and cook on low 4 to 8 hours or until set. Sprinkle cheese over top; cover and cook another 5 minutes or until cheese melts.

BARBECUE SANDWICH

1-1/2 pounds boneless beef round steak
1/2 teaspoon salt
1/4 teaspoon pepper
2 cups purchased coleslaw mix
1/2 cup barbecue sauce

Trim beef and cut into 1-inch pieces; sprinkle with salt and pepper. In a medium bowl, combine coleslaw mix and barbecue sauce, and mix to combine. Layer beef and coleslaw mixture in a slow cooker. Cover slow cooker and cook on low for 8 to 9 hours, until beef is tender. Stir well with fork so beef falls apart. Serve on crusty sandwich buns.

CHILI BEEF SANDWICHES

1 (3-pound) boneless beef chuck roast
1 package taco seasoning mix
1/2 cup barbecue sauce
8 Kaiser rolls, split and toasted

Trim excess fat from beef, and brown beef on all sides in heavy skillet over medium-high heat; transfer to a slow cooker. Sprinkle with seasoning mix and pour sauce over; cover and cook on low for 8 to 10 hours. Remove beef from slow cooker and shred; return to slow cooker. Make sandwiches with Kaiser rolls.

Cajun Beef and Potatoes

3 tablespoons Caribbean jerk marinade
1-1/2 pounds round steak
4 potatoes, cut into chunks
1/3 cup flour
1 (14-ounce) can diced tomatoes, undrained

Trim excess fat from round steak and cut into 1-inch pieces. Combine marinade and beef in a large glass dish and stir to coat. Let stand for 15 to 30 minutes. Place potatoes in a slow cooker. Add flour to marinade/beef mixture, mix to coat, and place on top of potatoes. Add undrained tomatoes. Cover and cook on low for 8 to 9 hours until beef and potatoes are tender.

Cheeseburgers

1 pound extra lean ground beef
3 tablespoons ketchup
2 teaspoons yellow mustard
2 cups pasteurized process American cheese, cubed
10 hamburger buns

Cook ground beef in a large skillet until thoroughly cooked, about 5 minutes. Stir frequently to break meat up into small pieces. Drain beef thoroughly.

Put cooked beef in a slow cooker with ketchup and mustard; mix well. Top with cubed cheese. Cover slow cooker and cook on low for 3 to 4 hours. Stir beef mixture gently. Serve in hamburger buns. Makes 10 servings.

Chuck Roast Au Gratin

6 potatoes, peeled and cut into quarters
3-1/2 pounds boned chuck roast
1 tablespoon dried chives, chopped (optional)
2 cans cream of mushroom soup
1/2 cup grated cheddar cheese
paprika

Place potatoes in the bottom of a slow cooker. Place roast over the top of the potatoes. Combine the chives with the soup and pour over top of roast. Cover and cook on low for 8 hours. Sprinkle with cheese and paprika. Cover and cook until cheese melts.

Meatloaf

1 pound lean ground beef
1/4 pound pork sausage
1/2 cup onions, chopped
1/2 cup bell pepper, chopped
salt and pepper, to taste
1 tablespoon ground sage
1 teaspoon garlic powder
1 tablespoon paprika
2 eggs
1/4 cup milk

Combine all ingredients and shape into a loaf. Place loaf on a trivet in the bottom of a slow cooker. Cover and cook on high about 4 hours or on low for 8 to 12 hours. Makes 6 servings.

MEATBALLS

1-1/2 pounds ground beef
1 can evaporated milk
1 cup quick cooking oatmeal
1 cup onion, finely chopped
1 egg
1/4 teaspoon garlic powder
1/4 teaspoon salt
1/4 teaspoon pepper
1 teaspoon chili powder
1 cup ketchup
3/4 cup brown sugar
1/4 teaspoon garlic powder
1 teaspoon liquid smoke

Mix ground beef, evaporated milk, oatmeal, onion, and egg together.
Mix in garlic powder, salt, pepper, and chili powder. Shape into
walnut-sized meatballs. Place meatballs in bottom of a slow cooker.
Mix together ketchup, brown sugar, garlic powder, and liquid smoke;
pour over meatballs. Cover and cook on low for 8 hours.

OLD-FASHIONED POT ROAST

6 small potatoes
6 small onions
6 medium carrots
1 (3-pound) boneless beef chuck roast
salt and pepper, to taste
1 cup water

Place all ingredients in a slow cooker in the order listed. Cover and
cook on low for 8 hours.

CORNED BEEF AND CABBAGE

4 cups hot water
2 tablespoons cider vinegar
2 tablespoons sugar
1/2 teaspoon black pepper
1 onion, cooked and cut into wedges
2-1/4 pounds whole corned beef brisket
8 small potatoes, scrubbed and quartered
1 head green cabbage, cored and cut into wedges

Combine first five ingredients in a slow cooker on high heat. Mix thoroughly. Add meat and potatoes. Cover and cook 4 hours. Remove lid and add cabbage wedges. Cover and cook another 3 to 4 hours, or until meat is tender. Carve beef into slices and serve with cabbage, potatoes, and sauce.

BEEF BURGUNDY

2-1/4 pounds boneless beef for stew
1 (11-ounce) can cream of celery soup
1 (11-ounce) can cream of chicken soup
1 (11-ounce) can cream of mushroom soup
1 package dry onion soup mix
1/2 cup beef broth

Combine all ingredients in a slow cooker on low heat. Cover and cook 8 hours. Serve over rice or noodles.

FRENCH ONION BEEF

1-1/4 pounds boneless beef round steak, cut into 1-inch cubes
1 cup fresh mushrooms, sliced
1 large onion, sliced
1 can condensed French onion soup
6 (1/4-ounce) package 15-minute stuffing mix
1/4 cup margarine or butter, melted
1/2 cup Mozzarella cheese, shredded

Place beef, mushrooms, and onion in bottom of a slow cooker. Pour soup on top. Cover and cook on low for 8 to 10 hours. Mix stuffing mix and contents of seasoning packet with melted margarine and 1/2 cup liquid from pot. Place stuffing in a slow cooker. Cover. Increase heat to high setting and cook for 10 minutes or until stuffing is fluffy. Sprinkle with cheese; cover. Cook until cheese is melted.

CRANBERRY PORK ROAST

4 potatoes, peeled and cut into 1-inch chunks
3 pounds boneless center-cut pork loin roast, rolled and tied
1 (16-ounce) can whole berry cranberry sauce
1 (5-ounce) can apricot nectar
1 cup pearl onions
1/2 cup dried apricots, coarsely chopped
1/2 cup sugar
1 teaspoon dry mustard
1/4 teaspoon crushed red pepper

Place the potatoes in the bottom of a slow cooker, then place the roast over the potatoes. In a large bowl, combine the remaining ingredients; mix well and pour over roast. Cover and cook on low for 5 to 6 hours. Remove the roast to a cutting board and thinly slice. Serve with the potatoes and sauce.

PORK WITH FRUIT

2 pounds boneless pork loin roast
1-1/2 cups mixed dried fruit
1/2 cup apple juice
1/2 teaspoon salt
1/4 teaspoon pepper

Place pork in a slow cooker and top with fruit. Pour apple juice over pork and sprinkle with salt and pepper. Cover slow cooker and cook on low for 7 to 9 hours until pork is tender.

MEXICAN PORK

1 pound boneless pork loin roast, cut into 1-inch pieces
1 (20-ounce) jar chunky salsa
1 (15-ounce) can pinto beans, rinsed and drained

Mix pork and salsa in a slow cooker and cover. Cook on low for 6 to 8 hours until pork is tender. Add beans, cover slow cooker, and cook 10 to 15 minutes until hot.

BABYBACK RIBS

1/4 cup chili powder
1/4 cup dark brown sugar
4 (1-pound) racks baby back ribs
1/4 cup favorite barbecue sauce or sweet and sour sauce

Mix chili powder and brown sugar; rub on ribs. Curl racks, meaty side out; stand upright on thick ends in 5 to 6-quart slow cooker. Cover and cook on low for 7 to 8 hours, or on high for 3 to 3-1/2 hours, or until meat is very tender.

Remove ribs to cutting board. Let rest for 5 minutes and brush with barbecue or sweet and sour sauce. Serve.

SWEET BARBECUE RIBS

3-1/2 pounds pork loin back ribs
1/2 teaspoon salt
1/4 teaspoon pepper
1/2 cup cola beverage
2/3 cup barbecue sauce

Cut ribs into 2 or 3 rib portions and place in slow cooker. Sprinkle with salt and pepper, and pour cola over. Cover slow cooker and cook on low for 8 to 9 hours until the ribs are tender. Drain liquid and discard. Pour barbecue sauce into a slow cooker and mix so ribs are coated. Cover slow cooker and cook on low for 1 hour until ribs are glazed.

PORK IN A BUN

1 (3 to 4-pound) pork butt, well trimmed
salt and pepper
2 onions, chopped
1 (16-ounce) jar prepared barbecue sauce
buns

Trim visible fat from the pork and season it with salt and pepper. Place the onions in a slow cooker; place the meat on top.

Pour 1/2 cup barbecue sauce over the meat. Cover slow cooker and cook on low for 9 to 10 hours. Remove the cooked meat from the slow cooker. Drain the juices from the pot, reserving the onions. Coarsely shred the meat into chunks, using two forks. Put the shredded meat and onions back in the slow cooker, mix in the remaining barbecue sauce, and cover and cook on low for about one hour. Serve.

HONEY BARBECUE PORK AND CARROTS

3 pounds boneless pork roast
1 (16-ounce) bag baby carrots
1/2 cup barbecue sauce
1/4 cup honey
1/2 teaspoon salt
1/4 teaspoon pepper

Place pork and carrots in a slow cooker. Combine barbecue sauce, honey, salt, and pepper in a small bowl, and pour over ingredients in slow cooker. Cover and cook on low for 8 to 10 hours or until pork is thoroughly cooked.

Polish Kraut and Apples

1 pound fresh or canned sauerkraut
1 pound lean smoked Polish sausage
3 tart cooking apples, thickly sliced
1/2 cup packed brown sugar
3/4 teaspoon salt
1/8 teaspoon pepper
1/2 teaspoon caraway seeds (optional)
3/4 cup apple juice or cider

Rinse sauerkraut and squeeze dry. Place half of the sauerkraut in a slow cooker. Cut sausage into 2-inch lengths. Place in a slow cooker. Continue to layer in slow cooker, in order, apples, brown sugar, salt, pepper and, if desired, caraway seeds. Top with remaining sauerkraut. Add apple juice. Do not stir. Cover and cook on high for 3 to 3-1/2 hours or on low for 6 to 7 hours, or until apples are tender. Stir before serving.

Caribbean Ribs

1 teaspoon pepper
1/2 teaspoon allspice
1 teaspoon ground mustard
1 teaspoon salt
3 pounds pork loin back ribs, cut into 4-inch pieces
1/2 cup water
1-1/2 cups barbecue sauce

Combine all spices in a small bowl. Rub ribs with spice mixture. Place in a slow cooker and pour water over. Cover and cook on low for 8 to 9 hours, or until ribs are tender when pierced with a fork.

Remove ribs from slow cooker and discard cooking liquid. Put ribs back in slow cooker and add barbecue sauce. Cover and cook on low for 1 hour.

EASIEST PORK CHOPS

4 pork chops, well trimmed
1 package onion soup mix
1 (10-ounce) can chicken broth

Brown the pork chops if you wish in a non-stick skillet, 3 to 4 minutes on each side. Place pork chops in a slow cooker. In a medium bowl, combine soup mix and chicken broth and stir until blended.

Pour this mixture over the pork chops. Cover slow cooker and cook on low heat for 6 to 8 hours.

PIZZA FONDUE

1/4 pound Italian sausage
1 onion, cooked and chopped
1 clove garlic, minced
2 pounds spaghetti sauce, without meat
1 cup fresh mushrooms, cooked and sliced
1-1/2 cups pepperoni, chopped
1 teaspoon oregano, crushed
Italian bread, for dipping

Sauté sausage, onion, and garlic in a skillet over medium-high heat until meat is browned. Drain and discard fat. Combine spaghetti sauce, mushrooms, pepperoni, and oregano in a slow cooker. Stir in meat mixture. Cover and cook on low 3 hours.

CANTONESE PORK

1-1/2 pounds pork steak, cubed
1 green onion, sliced
1 (4-ounce) can mushrooms, drained
1 onion, sliced
2 teaspoons Worcestershire sauce
1 (8-ounce) can tomato sauce
2 tablespoons brown sugar
1-1/2 tablespoons vinegar
cooked rice

Put all of the ingredients except the rice into a slow cooker. Cover and cook on low for 8 to 10 hours or on high for 4 to 6 hours. Serve over rice.

HAM AND SCALLOPED POTATOES

2 pounds ham, chopped into bite sized chunks
6 medium potatoes, peeled and thinly sliced
2 medium onions, peeled and chopped
1 can cream of mushroom soup
2 cups Colby cheese, shredded

Combine ham with potatoes and onions, and place in the bottom of a slow cooker. Pour cream of mushroom soup over the top. Cover and cook on low for 6 to 8 hours. About an hour before serving, stir in cheese.

PORK CHOPS AND APPLESAUCE

6 boneless pork chops, browned
salt and pepper, to taste
1/4 cup applesauce
1/4 cup brown sugar
1/2 teaspoon ground cinnamon
1 (8-ounce) can tomato sauce
1/4 cup vinegar

Salt and pepper pork chops to taste, place in a slow cooker. Place applesauce on top of the chops, then pour mixture over. Cover and cook on low for 4 to 6 hours.

CHUTNEY HAM

3 pounds boneless ham, fully cooked
1/4 teaspoon pepper
2 (6-ounce) jars mango chutney
1 onion, chopped
1 tablespoon balsamic vinegar

Place ham in a slow cooker. Mix remaining ingredients in a medium bowl and pour over the ham. Cover slow cooker and cook on low for 6 to 8 hours, until thoroughly heated.

APPLEY KIELBASA

2 pounds fully cooked kielbasa sausage
3/4 cup brown sugar
1 cup chunky applesauce
2 garlic cloves, minced

Cut kielbasa into 1-inch pieces and combine with brown sugar, applesauce, and garlic in a slow cooker. Cover and cook on low for 6 to 8 hours, until thoroughly heated. Makes 12 servings.

SWEET AND SPICY KIELBASA

1 cup brown sugar
1 tablespoon spicy mustard
2 pounds smoked kielbasa, fully cooked and cut into 1-inch pieces

Combine brown sugar and mustard in a slow cooker; add kielbasa, and stir evenly to coat. Cover slow cooker and cook on low 2-1/2 to 3 hours, stirring occasionally, until kielbasa is thoroughly heated. Makes 12 servings.

CHEESY SAUSAGE AND TORTELLINI

1 pound Italian sausage
1 (26-ounce) jar pasta sauce
1 (14-ounce) can diced tomatoes with Italian seasonings,
  undrained
1 (9-ounce) package refrigerated cheese tortellini
1 cup Parmesan cheese, grated

Cook sausage in a heavy skillet over medium heat until browned,
about 10 minutes. Stir sausage frequently to break up as it cooks.
Drain well and place in a slow cooker. Add pasta sauce and tomatoes,
and stir well. Cover and cook on low 7 to 8 hours. Then stir in
tortellini, cover again, and cook on low for 30 to 40 minutes until
pasta is tender and heated. Sprinkle with cheese and let stand 5
minutes before serving. Makes 4 servings.

ITALIAN PORK CHOPS

6 (1-inch-thick) boneless pork loin chops
salt and pepper, to taste
1 tablespoon olive oil
1 onion, chopped
2 cups chunky pasta sauce
1 cup Mozzarella cheese, shredded

Trim any excess fat from pork chops and sprinkle with salt and
pepper. Cook chops in olive oil in a heavy skillet over medium heat
until browned, about five minutes, turning once during cooking. Place
in a slow cooker. Top with onion and pasta sauce. Cover slow cooker
and cook on low for 4 to 6 hours until pork is tender and thoroughly
cooked. Top with cheese just before serving.

HONEY MUSTARD PORK ROAST

2 apples
1 onion, chopped
3 tablespoons honey mustard
1/4 teaspoon salt
1/4 teaspoon pepper
1 (2-pound) rolled boneless pork roast
1 tablespoon cornstarch
2 tablespoons water

Peel apples and cut into 1-inch pieces. In a slow cooker, mix onion and apples. Spread honey mustard over pork roast and sprinkle with salt and pepper. Place coated roast on top of onions and apples. Cover slow cooker and cook on low for 7 to 8 hours. Remove roast and cover with foil to keep warm. Combine cornstarch and water in a medium saucepan and blend with wire whisk. Add juices, apples, and onions from the slow cooker to saucepan, and cook over medium heat until mixture boils and thickens, stirring frequently. Serve roast with sauce. Makes 8 servings.

PINEAPPLE GINGER PORK

2 pounds boneless pork shoulder
2 tablespoons cooking oil
3/4 cup chicken broth
3 tablespoons quick-cooking tapioca
3 tablespoons low-sodium soy sauce
3 tablespoons oyster sauce (optional)
1 teaspoon fresh ginger, grated
1 (15-1/4-ounce) can pineapple chunks
4 medium carrots, cut into 1/2-inch slices
1 large onion, cut into 1-inch pieces
1 (8-ounce) can sliced water chestnuts, drained
1-1/2 cups fresh snow pea pods
3 cups hot cooked rice

Trim fat from pork. Cut pork into 1-inch cubes. In a large skillet, brown half of pork at a time in hot oil. Drain fat.

In a slow cooker, combine chicken broth, tapioca, soy sauce, oyster sauce, and ginger. Drain pineapple, reserving juice. Stir juice into broth mixture; cover and chill pineapple chunks. Add carrots, onion, and water chestnuts to cooker. Add pork. Cover and cook on low 6 to 8 hours or on high 3 to 4 hours.

If using a low heat setting, turn to high heat setting. Stir pineapple chunks and snow peas into cooker. Cover and cook 10 to 15 minutes more on high heat setting, or until peas are crisp-tender. Serve over rice. Makes 6 to 8 servings.

Tender Pork Roast

1 (3 to 4-pound) pork roast
1/2 cup apple juice
1 teaspoon dry mustard
1 teaspoon basil
1/2 teaspoon onion powder
1/2 cup soy sauce

Place roast in a slow cooker. Combine remaining ingredients and pour over roast. Cover and cook on low for 8 hours.

Ham and Beans

3/4 cup dry beans, mixed
3/4 cup soybeans
1 cup carrots, diced
1 cup celery, diced
1 cup onion, chopped
2 cups ham, chopped
2 teaspoons salt
2 tablespoons parsley flakes
1/2 teaspoon thyme

Soak dry beans overnight in water. The next day, cook for 4 hours in a slow cooker. Add remaining ingredients and cook 2 to 3 more hours until done. Add more water as needed.

HAM BALLS

1 pound ground beef
1-1/2 pounds ground ham
1 pound ground pork
1 cup milk
2-1/2 cups bread crumbs
2 eggs, well-beaten
Sauce:
1 cup brown sugar
1 teaspoon mustard
1/2 cup vinegar
1/2 cup water

Combine all meatball ingredients well and form into golf ball-sized balls. Place in the bottom of a slow cooker. Mix sauce ingredients together and pour over meatballs. Cover and cook for 8 to 10 hours.

ISLAND RIBS

2-1/2 pounds country-style pork loin ribs
1/4 cup onion, finely chopped
1/4 cup barbecue sauce
1 teaspoon orange peel, grated
1 teaspoon lime peel, grated
1/2 teaspoon salt
1/4 cup orange juice
1 tablespoon lime juice

Place ribs in a slow cooker. In a small bowl, combine all remaining ingredients; mix well and pour over ribs. Cover; cook on low for 7 to 9 hours. Spoon sauce over ribs.

Polynesian Spareribs

3 to 4 pounds pork spareribs
5 tablespoons sugar
3 tablespoons honey
3 tablespoons soy sauce
2 tablespoons ketchup
1 teaspoon seasoning salt
1 cup chicken broth

Place ribs in the bottom of a slow cooker. Mix remaining ingredients and pour over ribs. Cover and cook on low for 8 to 9 hours. If the ribs are fatty, boil them for 5 minutes before placing in the slow cooker.

Pineapple Bean pot

2 pounds canned pinto beans, rinsed and drained
1 pound canned black beans, rinsed and drained
1 pound Texas-style barbecue beans, undrained
1-1/4 pounds unsweetened pineapple chunks, drained
1/3 cup barbecue sauce
2 tablespoons prepared mustard
1 onion, cooked and chopped
1 green bell pepper, cooked, seeded, and chopped
1 pound cooked ham, cut into 3/4-inch cubes
2 tablespoons apple cider vinegar

Combine first nine ingredients in a slow cooker on low heat. Mix gently. Cover and cook 5-1/2 to 6 hours. Stir in vinegar and pepper to taste before serving.

SMOKED SAUSAGE AND POTATOES

1 (10-1/2-ounce) can condensed beef broth
1 cup water
1/8 teaspoon pepper
2 medium onions, quartered
6 carrots, julienned
1-1/2 cup celery, diced
2 potatoes, pared and diced
2 tablespoons water
1 pound smoked sausage

Combine broth, water, and all vegetables except potatoes in a slow cooker. Cover and cook for 1 hour on low. Add potatoes. Cover and cook for 6 hours on low. Add sausage and cook for an additional hour.

RED BEANS AND RICE

1 pound dried red kidney beans
1 cup cooked ham pieces
1 onion, chopped
1 tablespoon Worcestershire sauce
1 teaspoon Tabasco sauce
2 bay leaves
2 garlic cloves, minced
4 tablespoons parsley
4 cups water
hot cooked rice

Soak red beans overnight in enough water to cover beans. The next day, drain beans and place in a slow cooker. Add ham and all other seasonings. Pour water over all and cook on low for 8 hours or until beans are tender. Serve over rice.

LAMB SHANKS

4 lamb shanks, fat trimmed
3/4 cup hot water
2 teaspoons prepared mustard
2 cubes beef bouillon
2 teaspoons horseradish sauce
2 garlic cloves, minced
3 tablespoons apple or mint jelly
2 tablespoons lemon juice

Prepare broiler. Broil lamb 4 inches from heat source to brown on all sides. Transfer lamb to a slow cooker. Add remaining ingredients and stir well. Cover and cook on low 8 hours or on high 4 hours.

POULTRY

JAMBALAYA

1 pound boneless chicken thighs, cut into 1-inch pieces
3 celery stalks, chopped
1 green bell pepper, chopped
2 onions, chopped
3 garlic cloves, minced
1 (28-ounce) can crushed tomatoes, undrained
1 tablespoon sugar
1/2 teaspoon dried oregano leaves
1/2 teaspoon dried basil leaves
1/2 cup rice, uncooked
1 pound frozen cooked shrimp, thawed

Combine all ingredients except rice and shrimp in a slow cooker. Cover and cook on low for 7 to 9 hours until chicken is cooked through. Increase heat to high. Stir in rice, cover, and cook for 15 minutes, or until is tender. Add shrimp, stir, cover, and cook an additional 3 to 5 minutes until shrimp are heated through. Makes 6 servings.

CHICKEN STROGANOFF

1 cup light sour cream
1 tablespoon flour
1 (1-ounce) package chicken gravy mix
1 cup water
1 pound boneless, skinless chicken breasts
1 pound bag frozen mixed vegetables, thawed

In a slow cooker, mix sour cream, flour, gravy mix, and water; stir with wire whisk until well blended. Cut chicken breasts into 1-inch pieces and add to slow cooker. Stir in vegetables and cover. Cook on low for 4 hours until chicken is tender. Turn heat to high and cook for 1 hour longer until sauce is thickened and chicken is thoroughly cooked. Makes 4 servings.

SOUTH OF THE BORDER CHICKEN

4 boneless chicken breast halves
1 (10-ounce) can broccoli cheese soup
1/3 cup evaporated milk
4 cups hot cooked rice
salsa
sour cream
1 small avocado, sliced (optional)

Place chicken in the bottom of a slow cooker. Combine soup and milk; pour over chicken. Cover and cook on low for 7 to 8 hours. Serve with rice. Top with salsa, sour cream, and avocado.

KONA CHICKEN

3 pounds chicken, chopped
1/2 cup green onions, chopped
1/2 cup soy sauce
1/4 cup chicken broth
1/2 cup water
1/2 cup honey

Place chicken in a slow cooker. Mix together onions, soy sauce, chicken broth, and water. Pour over top of chicken. Cover and cook on low until chicken is tender, 3 to 5 hours. Remove chicken from slow cooker. Brush with honey and place in broiler. Broil until golden brown, brushing with honey several times. Serve with sauce from slow cooker.

ONION AND MUSHROOM CHICKEN

2-1/2 to 3 pounds chicken, cut up
1 package onion mushroom soup
1/2 teaspoon salt
1/4 teaspoon thyme
1 garlic clove, minced
1-1/2 cups beef broth
1/2 cup water
1 can small onions, drained
2 tablespoons parsley, chopped

Place the chicken in a slow cooker. Mix together all remaining ingredients and pour over chicken. Cover and cook on low for 8 hours.

LEMON CHICKEN

1/2 pounds chicken breasts, boneless and skinless
salt and pepper, to taste
juice of half of a lemon

Place chicken in a slow cooker. Squeeze lemon juice over the chicken. Sprinkle with salt and pepper. Cover and cook on low for 6 to 8 hours. Add more lemon juice if needed.

LEMON PEPPER CHICKEN

5 chicken breasts, boneless and skinless
lemon pepper seasoning
2 teaspoons butter, melted

Sprinkle chicken breasts with lemon pepper seasoning to taste. Place chicken in a slow cooker. Pour butter over top of chicken. Cover and cook on low for 8 to 10 hours.

LIME CHICKEN

4 chicken cutlets
1/4 cup lime juice
2 tablespoons olive oil
1/2 teaspoon oregano
1/2 teaspoon garlic salt

Combine all ingredients in a slow cooker. Cover and cook on low for 8 hours. Add liquid if necessary.

BROWN SUGAR CHICKEN

2 pounds boneless chicken pieces
1 cup packed brown sugar
2/3 cup vinegar
1/4 cup lemon lime soda
2 tablespoons garlic, minced
2 tablespoons soy sauce
1 teaspoon black pepper
cooked rice

Place chicken pieces in a slow cooker. Combine remaining ingredients and pour over the top of chicken. Cover and cook on low for 6 to 8 hours. Serve with rice. Makes 4 servings.

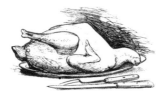

GARLIC PEPPER CHICKEN

4 chicken leg quarters
2 tablespoons garlic, minced
2 teaspoons pepper
1 can zucchini with tomato sauce
1/2 cup Mozzarella cheese, shredded

Place chicken in a slow cooker. Sprinkle with garlic and pepper. Pour zucchini with tomato sauce over chicken. Cook for 6 hours on high. Sprinkle with cheese and cook until cheese melts, about 30 minutes.

CURRIED CHICKEN

3 to 4 chicken breasts
1/2 cup honey
1/2 cup Dijon-style mustard
2 tablespoons soy sauce
1/4 tablespoon curry powder

Place all ingredients in a slow cooker. Cover and cook on low for 8 hours.

SUNSHINE CHICKEN

8 skinless, boneless chicken breasts
1 cup barbecue sauce
1 cup orange juice

Place chicken breasts in a slow cooker. Combine BBQ sauce with orange juice. Pour over the chicken breasts. Cover and cook on low for 8 hours.

ORANGE CHICKEN

1/2 teaspoon salt
1/2 teaspoon chili powder
1/2 teaspoon ground cayenne pepper
1/2 teaspoon paprika
4 boneless, skinless chicken breasts
1 cup onion, chopped
1/2 cup bell pepper, chopped
1/2 cup celery, chopped
2 garlic cloves, minced
3/4 cup orange juice
1 teaspoon orange peel, grated
2 tablespoons honey
1 tablespoon Worcestershire sauce
1/2 teaspoon ground ginger

Combine salt, cayenne pepper, chili powder, and paprika. Sprinkle over chicken. Set aside. Place onion, bell pepper, celery, and garlic in the bottom of a slow cooker. Place chicken on top. Mix orange juice, peel, honey, Worcestershire sauce, and ginger. Pour over chicken. Cook for 6 to 8 hours on low.

Smothered Chicken and Vegetables

3 carrots, sliced
3 celery stalks, sliced
1 large onion, cut into thin wedges
3 cups chicken, cooked and cubed
1 (10-ounce) can condensed cream of celery soup
3/4 cup chicken broth

Place vegetables in the bottom of a slow cooker. Top with chicken. Add soup and broth. Cover and cook for 4 to 6 hours on low.

Chicken Tacos

1 fryer chicken, skinned if desired
1 (18-ounce) jar salsa
2 tablespoons taco seasoning mix

Place chicken in a slow cooker. In a medium bowl, combine salsa and taco seasoning and mix to blend. Pour over the chicken, cover slow cooker, and cook on low for 6 to 8 hours, until chicken is tender and thoroughly cooked. Remove skin and bones from chicken. Shred meat and stir back into liquid in slow cooker. Cook 20 to 30 minutes longer, until thoroughly heated. Serve in tacos or sandwiches.

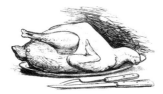

SPICY CHICKEN

1 (3-pound) whole chicken
1 medium potato, peeled and sliced
2 onions, finely chopped
4 to 7 garlic cloves, minced
2 bay leaves
1 teaspoon ground cumin
1 teaspoon oregano
1 tablespoon chili powder
2 cups soft white bread crumbs
2 chicken bouillon cubes
1-3/4 cups water
cilantro, for garnish

Wash chicken inside and out, and place in a slow cooker. Place potato slices around bottom sides of pot. Add onions, garlic, spices, and bread crumbs, pushing the crumbs down around the chicken. Microwave bouillon cubes with water and pour over the chicken. Cover and cook on low heat 7 hours, or high heat for 4 hours.

Remove lid and let cool for about 20 minutes. Carefully lift chicken onto a plate using two wide-slotted spoons. Remove and discard bay leaves, skin, and bones. When sauce is very warm (not hot), use a slotted spoon to check for remaining bones. Then pour sauce into a food processor or blender and process until smooth. Serve chicken with sauce, and garnish with cilantro.

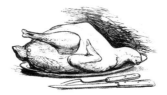

CHICKEN CORDON BLEU

6 boneless skinless chicken breasts
6 pieces Swiss cheese
6 slices ham
1 (10-ounce) can condensed cream of mushroom soup with
  roasted garlic
3 tablespoons water
1/4 teaspoon pepper

Flatten each chicken breast with a wooden mallet or rolling pin. Place a piece of cheese and a slice of ham in the center of each. Fold up and secure with toothpicks. Place in a slow cooker. Combine remaining ingredients and pour over chicken bundles, making sure pieces are fully covered.

Cover and cook on low 6 to 7 hours.

CHEESY CHICKEN

6 boneless, skinless chicken breasts
1 (10-ounce) can condensed cream of chicken soup
1 (10-ounce) can condensed fiesta cheese soup
cooked rice or noodles

Place chicken breasts in a slow cooker. Pour the undiluted soups over the chicken and stir to combine. Cover and cook on low 6 to 8 hours, until chicken is tender and thoroughly cooked. Serve over rice or noodles.

Peanut Chicken

3-1/2 pounds boneless, skinless chicken breasts
1/3 cup peanut butter
2 tablespoons low sodium soy sauce
3 tablespoons orange juice
1/8 teaspoon pepper
cooked rice or noodles

Combine all ingredients in a slow cooker; mix well. Cover and cook on low for 6 to 8 hours, or until chicken is tender and thoroughly cooked. Serve with hot cooked rice or noodles.

Sweet and Sour Chicken

2 pounds boneless, skinless chicken thighs
1 (26-ounce) jar sweet and sour simmer sauce
1 (16-ounce) package frozen broccoli, carrots, and peppers,
  thawed and drained

Cut chicken thighs into 1-1/2-inch pieces. Mix with simmer sauce in slow cooker. Cover and cook on low setting for 8 to 10 hours, or until chicken is tender and no longer pink. Ten to 15 minutes before serving, stir in vegetables. Cover, increase heat to high, and cook for 10 to 15 minutes, or until vegetables are crisp-tender.

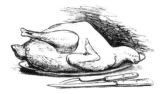

Chicken Wings

5 pounds chicken wings, cut into 3 pieces
2 cups brown sugar
1/2 cup mustard
1/2 cup ketchup
1/4 cup Worcestershire sauce

Put chicken in a slow cooker. Combine remaining ingredients and pour over chicken. Cook on low for 6 to 8 hours. Makes 10 servings.

Italian Chicken

1-1/2 pounds boneless, skinless chicken breasts
1/2 cup zesty Italian salad dressing
1/8 teaspoon pepper
4 garlic cloves, minced
4 potatoes, cubed

Combine all ingredients in a slow cooker. Cover and cook on low for 6 to 8 hours until chicken is thoroughly cooked and potatoes are tender.

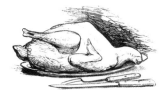

COLA CHICKEN

1 whole chicken
1 cup ketchup
1 cup cola

Place whole chicken in a slow cooker on low heat. Pour ketchup and cola over chicken. Cook on low 9 hours.

CHICKEN MARENGO

1 whole chicken, cut up
2 (1-ounce) packages spaghetti sauce mix
1/2 cup apple cider vinegar
1/2 cup chicken broth
2 fresh tomatoes, quartered
1/4 pound fresh mushrooms

Place chicken parts in bottom of a slow cooker. Combine spaghetti sauce mix, vinegar, and broth; pour over chicken. Cover and cook on low 6 to 7 hours. Turn control to high. Add tomatoes and mushrooms. Cover and cook on high for 30 to 40 minutes, or until tomatoes are done. Makes 4 to 5 servings.

Orange-glazed Chicken

1/2 cup orange marmalade
1/3 cup bottled Russian dressing
1/2 package onion soup mix
6 frozen chicken breasts, unthawed

Mix the first three ingredients together. Place chicken in a slow cooker and cover with marmalade mixture. Cover and cook on low 6 to 8 hours.

Aloha Chicken

1/3 cup steak sauce
2 tablespoons honey
1 (8-ounce) can pineapple chunks, drained, reserve 2 tablespoons juice
1 medium green bell pepper, chopped
4 chicken breast halves, boneless and skinless

Mix steak sauce with honey and reserved pineapple juice. Place green peppers in the bottom of a slow cooker. Add chicken breasts on top. Pour honey mixture over the chicken breasts. Cover and cook on low for 4 to 6 hours. Add pineapple chunks and cook an additional 30 to 60 minutes.

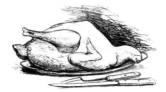

SOUR CREAM AND BACON CHICKEN

8 bacon slices
8 boneless, skinless chicken breasts
2 (10-ounce) cans roasted garlic cream of mushroom soup
1 cup sour cream
1/2 cup flour

Wrap one slice of bacon around each boneless chicken breast and place in a slow cooker. In a medium bowl, combine condensed soups, sour cream, and flour, then mix with wire whisk to blend. Pour over chicken. Cover and cook on low for 6 to 8 hours until chicken and bacon are thoroughly cooked. Makes 8 servings.

PEACHY CHICKEN

4 boneless, skinless chicken thighs
2 sweet potatoes, peeled and cubed
1 onion, chopped
2 tablespoons water
3 tablespoons cornstarch
1/2 cup peach preserves

Put chicken in a slow cooker and top with sweet potatoes and onions. Cover and cook on low for 7 to 8 hours, until chicken is thoroughly cooked and sweet potatoes are tender when pierced with fork. Remove chicken, sweet potatoes, and onions from slow cooker with a slotted spoon and cover with foil to keep warm.

In a heavy saucepan, combine water and cornstarch and mix well. Add juices from slow cooker along with preserves. Cook and stir over medium heat, stirring frequently, until mixture boils and thickens. Cook for 2 minutes, then pour over chicken and vegetables.

CHICKEN DINNER

1 fresh whole frying chicken, rinsed, giblets removed
8 large carrots, cooked, peeled, and cut into 2-inch pieces
6 potatoes, peeled and sliced
1 package dry onion soup mix
1 teaspoon basil
1 cup chicken stock

Place chicken, carrots, and potatoes in a slow cooker. Combine remaining ingredients in a bowl and pour over. Cover and cook on high about 5 hours or on low about 9 hours, until chicken leg and thigh come off easily when pulled.

CHICKEN MEATBALLS

1 teaspoon paprika
1 teaspoon garlic powder
salt and pepper, to taste
3 pounds chicken breasts
1 (6-ounce) can tomato paste
1 cup water
1 (8-ounce) can mushrooms, sliced
cooked rice

Combine paprika, garlic powder, salt, and pepper. Sprinkle spice mixture on each piece of chicken. Place chicken in a slow cooker. Mix tomato paste and water together. Pour over the chicken. Add sliced mushrooms. Cover and cook on low for 7 to 9 hours. Serve over rice.

Lacquered Chicken

1 tablespoon vegetable oil
1 (2-pound) whole chicken
3 very large onions, peeled and chopped
5 large tomatoes, chopped
1 medium orange, unpeeled, seeded, chopped
1 teaspoon sugar
1 teaspoon salt
1/8 teaspoon pepper
1/2 cup water
1 bouillon cube, crumbled
3 tablespoons red currant, raspberry, or red grape jelly
1/4 cup apple cider

Heat the oil in a skillet and sauté the chicken, turning often, until well browned. Remove the chicken and set aside. Sauté onion in skillet until well browned. Put onions in the bottom of a slow cooker. Place tomatoes, orange, sugar, salt, and pepper in the pot, and set chicken on top. Add the water and bouillon cube. Cover and cook on low for 5 to 7 hours.

Before serving, remove the chicken to a deep serving dish and keep warm. Place the vegetables from the slow cooker into a skillet, and simmer until thick. Stir in the jelly and the apple cider and cook, stirring until the sauce boils. Do not over cook, lest the sauce lose its shiny quality. If sauce is not shiny enough, bring back to a very brisk boil and quickly stir in some jelly. Pour sauce over the chicken.

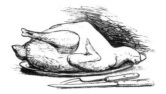

PIZZA CHICKEN

8 boneless, skinless chicken breasts
1/4 teaspoon salt
1/8 teaspoon pepper
1 onion, chopped
2 bell peppers, cut into 1-inch pieces
2 cups pasta sauce
1 cup Mozzarella cheese, shredded
cooked pasta or rice

Sprinkle chicken with salt and pepper and place in a slow cooker. Top with onions and bell peppers and pour pasta sauce over all. Cover slow cooker and cook on low 4 to 5 hours until chicken is thoroughly cooked. Stir well, then sprinkle with cheese and let stand 5 minutes to melt cheese. Serve over cooked pasta or rice. Makes 8 servings.

CREAMY ITALIAN CHICKEN

2 pounds boneless, skinless chicken breasts
1/4 cup butter, melted
1 (8-ounce) container cream cheese with chives, softened
1 (10-ounce) can condensed golden cream of mushroom soup
1 (7-ounce) package Italian dressing mix
1/2 cup water
cooked pasta or rice

Cut chicken breasts into strips and place into a slow cooker. In a medium bowl, combine butter, cream cheese, soup, Italian dressing mix, and water; stir until blended. Pour over chicken. Cover and cook on low for 6 to 8 hours. Stir well, then serve over hot cooked pasta or rice. Makes 4 to 6 servings.

Asian-spiced Chicken and Beans

1 pound canned navy beans, drained and rinsed
1 pound canned red beans, drained and rinsed
1 pound boneless, skinless chicken breasts, cut into 1/2-inch cubes
3 carrots, diagonally sliced
2-1/2 teaspoons garlic, minced
2-1/2 teaspoons fresh ginger root, minced, or 1-1/2 teaspoons
  ground ginger
1-3/4 cups low sodium chicken broth, fat-free, divided
2 tablespoons cornstarch
1/2 teaspoon red pepper, crushed
2-1/2 tablespoons low sodium soy sauce
4 cups rice, cooked

Place beans, chicken, carrots, garlic, ginger, and 1-1/4 cup chicken broth in a slow cooker; stir well. Cover and cook on low until ingredients are tender, about 5 hours.

Turn slow cooker to high. Stir in combined cornstarch and remaining chicken broth; stir in crushed red pepper. Cover and cook until thickened, about 30 minutes. Stir in soy sauce. Serve over rice.

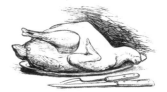

Vinegar Chicken

1 large chicken, cut up
2 tablespoons apple cider vinegar
1 tablespoon soy sauce
2 tablespoons oil
1/3 cup water
1/2 cube chicken bouillon
1 tablespoon brown sugar
1 teaspoon thyme
1/2 teaspoon salt
dash black pepper
2 garlic cloves, crushed (optional)
2 tablespoons chopped parsley

Place chicken in the bottom of a slow cooker. Mix remaining ingredients and pour over chicken. Cover and cook on low for 8 to 10 hours.

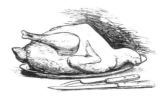

CHICKEN SPAGHETTI

2 pounds boneless, skinless chicken breasts or thighs
1 package dry spaghetti mix
2 garlic cloves, minced
2 onions, chopped
1 (14-ounce) can crushed tomatoes
1 (8-ounce) can tomato sauce
1 (6-ounce) can tomato paste
1/2 teaspoon crushed red pepper flakes
1/2 teaspoon Italian seasoning
1/2 teaspoon black pepper
1/2 teaspoon ground oregano
1 (16-ounce) package angel hair pasta, cooked
1 cup Mozzarella cheese, shredded

Place chicken in a slow cooker, followed by all other ingredients
except pasta and cheese. Cook on low for 6 to 8 hours. Near the end
of cooking time, break up chicken into small pieces and stir. Serve
over angel hair pasta and sprinkle with mozzarella cheese. Makes 6 to
8 servings.

CITRUS CHICKEN

3 garlic cloves, minced
2 tablespoons olive oil
1 (3-1/2-pound) whole chicken, cut up
3 bay leaves
1/2 cup water
1 cup orange juice
2 tablespoons lime juice
2 tablespoons coarsely ground black pepper
salt, to taste

Heat garlic in olive oil. Place chicken in the bottom of a slow cooker, then add remaining ingredients. Cover and cook on low for 8 hours.

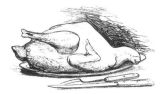

CHICKEN TORTILLAS

1 whole chicken, cooked and removed from bone
1 can cream of chicken soup
1/2 cup green chili salsa
2 tablespoons quick-cooking tapioca
1 dozen corn tortillas
1 medium onion, chopped
1-1/2 cup grated cheese
black olives, sliced

Tear chicken into bite size pieces; mix with soup, chili salsa, and tapioca. Line bottom of a slow cooker with 3 corn tortillas, torn into pieces. Add 1/3 of the chicken mixture. Sprinkle with 1/3 of the onion and 1/3 of the grated cheese. Repeat layers of tortillas topped with chicken mixture, onions, and cheese. Cover and cook on low 6 to 8 hours. Garnish with black olives.

ALMOND CHICKEN

6 boneless and skinless chicken breasts
1/2 cup chicken broth
1 can cream of mushroom soup
1/2 pint sour cream
almonds, sliced

Place the chicken breasts in the bottom of a slow cooker. Mix together the broth, soup, and sour cream. Pour over the chicken. Cover and cook for 8 hours on low heat. Sprinkle with almonds before serving.

TANGY CHICKEN THIGHS

2 pounds chicken thighs, boneless, skinless, and cut into 1-1/2-inch pieces
1 (14-ounce) can tomatoes, diced and undrained
1 (6-ounce) can tomato paste
1 onion, chopped
2 cups carrots, diced
1 tablespoon dried basil
1 teaspoon dried oregano
1/2 teaspoon dried thyme, crushed
1/2 teaspoon rosemary, crumbled
2 garlic cloves, crushed
1/2 teaspoon black pepper
1/2 cup fresh orange juice
1-1/2 teaspoons sugar
2 tablespoons orange peel, grated
2 tablespoons lemon juice
4 slices cooked bacon, crumbled

Combine first thirteen ingredients and half the orange zest in a slow cooker on low heat. Mix thoroughly. Cover and cook 6 to 6-1/2 hours, or until chicken is cooked throughout. Stir in lemon juice and remaining orange zest. Serve sprinkled with crumbled bacon.

Soy Chicken

1/2 cup vinegar
6 to 8 garlic cloves, crushed
1/2 teaspoon black peppercorns
1 bay leaf
1/2 tablespoon salt
2-1/2 tablespoons soy sauce
1/4 cup water
1 whole chicken, cut up

In a slow cooker combine vinegar, garlic, peppercorns, bay leaf, salt, and soy sauce. Add chicken. Cover and cook on high for one hour. Add water. Lower heat setting to low and cook for 4 to 5 hours.

CHICKEN WITH MUSHROOMS AND BASIL

3 cups fresh mushrooms, cooked and sliced
1 onion, cooked and chopped
2 garlic cloves, minced
salt and pepper
2-1/4 pounds skinless chicken pieces, rinsed
1 cup chicken stock
1 (6-ounce) can tomato paste
2 tablespoons quick cooking tapioca
2 teaspoons sugar
1-1/2 teaspoons dried basil, crushed
2 cups cooked noodles
2 tablespoons Parmesan cheese, grated

Combine first three ingredients, and salt and pepper to taste in a slow cooker. Arrange chicken pieces over vegetables. Combine stock, next four ingredients, and salt and pepper to taste in a bowl. Add dried basil. Pour over chicken. Cover and cook on low 7 to 8 hours or on high about 4 hours. Serve over noodles, sprinkled with Parmesan cheese.

TAVERNA CHICKEN

1 (4-pound) chicken, cut up
1 onion, chopped
2 garlic cloves, minced
1 green bell pepper, chopped
1 medium ripe tomato, peeled and chopped
1 cup chicken broth
pinch of cayenne pepper

Combine all ingredients in a slow cooker. Cover and cook on low for 6 to 8 hours.

Tennessee Breast of Chicken

4 chicken breast halves
1/4 cup flour
1/2 teaspoon paprika
salt and pepper
2 tablespoons butter
2 tablespoons oil
2 tablespoons onion, chopped
2 tablespoons parsley, chopped
1/4 teaspoon dried chervil
1/4 cup Dr. Pepper
1 (4-ounce) can mushrooms, undrained
1 (10-ounce) can tomatoes
1/4 teaspoon sugar
salt and pepper

Dredge chicken in flour that has been mixed with paprika and a little salt. Heat butter and oil in a skillet and sauté chicken on both sides until lightly browned. Stir in onion, parsley, and chervil, then cook briefly. Remove from heat. Place chicken in a slow cooker. Combine remaining ingredients and pour over chicken. Cover and cook on low for 6 to 7 hours. Serve with noodles or rice.

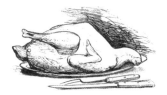

CHICKEN AND DUMPLINGS

4 boneless skinless chicken breasts, cut into small chunks
2 cans condensed cream of chicken soup
1/4 cup onion, finely diced
2 cups water
2 (10-ounce) packages refrigerated biscuits
1 chicken bouillon cube

Combine all ingredients, except biscuits, in a slow cooker. Cover and cook on low for 5 to 6 hours. Thirty minutes before serving, tear biscuit dough into 1-inch pieces. Add to the slow cooker, stirring gently. Cover and cook on high for an additional 30 minutes, or until biscuits are cooked through.

CHICKEN AND SHRIMP

1 (12-ounce) package chicken thighs, skinless and boneless
1 large onion, chopped
3 garlic cloves, minced
1 (14 1/2-ounce) can diced tomatoes, Italian style
2 tablespoons tomato paste
1/2 cup chicken broth
2 tablespoons lemon juice
2 bay leaves
1/2 teaspoon salt
1/4 teaspoon crushed red pepper
1/2 pound frozen peeled shrimp, thawed and drained
1/2 pound frozen artichoke hearts, thawed and coarsely chopped
2 cups pasta, cooked
1/2 cup crumbled feta cheese

Cut chicken thighs into quarters. Put onion and garlic in a slow cooker. Top with the chicken pieces. In a bowl, combine the undrained tomatoes, tomato paste, chicken broth, lemon juice, bay leaves, salt, and crushed red pepper. Pour over all. Cover; cook on low heat setting for 6 to 7 hours. Turn to high. Remove bay leaves. Stir in shrimp and artichoke hearts. Cover; cook for 5 minutes more. Serve chicken and shrimp mixture over hot cooked pasta. Sprinkle with feta cheese. Makes 4 servings.

ISLAND CHICKEN

1 (8-ounce) can pineapple chunks in heavy syrup
2 pounds chicken parts
1 can chicken broth
1/4 cup vinegar
2 tablespoons brown sugar
2 teaspoons soy sauce
1 garlic clove, minced
1 green bell pepper, cut in squares
3 tablespoons cornstarch
1/4 cup water

Drain pineapple and reserve liquid. Put chicken parts in bottom of a slow cooker. Mix together pineapple syrup, chicken broth, vinegar, brown sugar, and soy sauce in a saucepan. Heat until brown sugar dissolves. Pour over chicken. Heat on high for 1 hour. Add pineapple chunks, garlic, and green bell pepper. Cover and cook on low for 7 to 9 hours. Half an hour before serving, mix together cornstarch and water and add to the slow cooker.

CHICKEN DIVAN

1 package frozen broccoli spears
2 to 3 chicken breasts, boneless and skinless
1 can cream of chicken soup
1-1/4 cups mayonnaise
1 teaspoon lemon juice

Place broccoli in the bottom of a slow cooker. Put chicken on top of broccoli. Mix together soup, mayonnaise, and lemon juice. Pour over chicken, mixing slightly. Cover and cook on low for 8 hours.

CHICKEN CASSEROLE

1-1/2 pounds chicken breasts, boneless and skinless
6 carrots, sliced
1 can green beans
2 cans cream of mushroom soup
2 tablespoons mayonnaise
1/2 cup cheddar cheese, shredded

Place chicken in bottom of a slow cooker. Mix carrots, green beans, mushroom soup, and mayonnaise. Pour over chicken. Cover and cook for 8 to 10 hours on low. Sprinkle with cheddar cheese before serving.

CREAMY CHICKEN

6 to 8 chicken pieces
1 cup evaporated milk
1 can cream of mushroom soup
salt and pepper, to taste
paprika

Place chicken in a slow cooker. Mix together evaporated milk with soup. Pour over chicken. Sprinkle with salt, pepper, and paprika. Cover and cook on low for 8 hours.

Maple-glazed Turkey Breast

1 (6-ounce) package long grain wild rice mix
1-1/4 cups water
2 pounds boneless turkey breast, thawed if frozen
1/4 cup maple syrup
1 onion, chopped
1/4 teaspoon ground cinnamon
1/2 teaspoon salt
1/8 teaspoon white pepper

Combine rice, seasoning mix packet, and water in a slow cooker. Place turkey breast on top, sprinkle with onions, and drizzle with maple syrup. Sprinkle with cinnamon, salt, and pepper, then cover. Cook on low for 5 to 6 hours until turkey is thoroughly cooked and registers 180° on a meat thermometer. Makes 4 servings.

French Turkey

1-1/2 cups dried great Northern beans
1 pound turkey breast tenderloin
2 onions, chopped
1 (14-ounce) can chicken broth
1-1/2 cups water
1 (14-ounce) can diced tomatoes, undrained
1/8 teaspoon white pepper
1/4 teaspoon salt
1/2 teaspoon dried thyme leaves

Place beans in a medium bowl and cover with water. Cover and let stand overnight to soak. Drain beans and discard soaking water. Place beans in a slow cooker. Cut turkey into 1-inch pieces and place in a slow cooker along with onions, chicken broth, and water. Cover and cook on low for 8 to 10 hours. Stir in tomatoes and pepper. Cover again; cook on low for 30 minutes until hot. Makes 6 servings.

Home-style Turkey Dinner

3 medium Yukon gold potatoes, cut into 2-inch pieces
3 pounds turkey thighs, skin removed
1 (12-ounce) jar home style turkey gravy
2 tablespoons all-purpose flour
1 teaspoon parsley flakes
1/2 teaspoon dried thyme leaves
1/8 teaspoon freshly ground black pepper
1 (16-ounce) bag frozen baby green bean and carrot blend,
  thawed and drained
fresh thyme sprigs, for garnish
1 cup cranberry sauce

Place potatoes in a slow cooker. Arrange turkey thighs on top of potatoes. In a medium bowl, mix gravy, flour, herbs, and pepper until smooth. Pour mixture over turkey. Cover and cook on low for 8 to 10 hours, or until the internal temperature reaches 180°. Stir in vegetable blend and continue to cook in covered container on low for 30 more minutes or until vegetables are tender. Using a slotted spoon, remove turkey and vegetables from the slow cooker.

Stir sauce with a wooden spoon and serve with turkey. Garnish with fresh thyme and serve with cranberry sauce.

This recipe used by permission of the National Turkey Federation.

Turkey Teriyaki Sandwich

1-1/2 pounds boneless, skinless turkey thighs
1/2 cup teriyaki baste and glaze sauce
3 tablespoons orange marmalade
1/4 teaspoon pepper

Combine all ingredients in a slow cooker; cover and cook on low for 9 to 10 hours. Remove turkey from slow cooker, shred turkey using two forks, and return to slow cooker. Cook on high for 10 to 15 minutes until sauce is thickened. Serve on hoagie buns.

Southwest Turkey Loaf

2/3 cup salsa
1 egg, beaten
1/4 teaspoon pepper
1/4 teaspoon salt
1-1/4 pounds ground turkey

In a medium bowl, combine salsa, egg, pepper, and salt and mix well. Add ground turkey and combine. Form into a 6-inch round loaf and place loaf on a rack or balled up foil balls in a slow cooker. Cover slow cooker and cook on low for 4 to 5 hours, until turkey is thoroughly cooked.

CRANBERRY APPETIZER TURKEY ROUNDS

2 large eggs, well beaten
2 pounds ground turkey
1 cup dry bread crumbs
2 tablespoons minced sweet onion
2 garlic cloves, minced
1/3 cup minced fresh parsley
1/3 cup ketchup
2 tablespoons soy sauce
1/2 teaspoon salt
1/4 teaspoon black pepper
1 (16-ounce) can whole berry cranberry sauce
1-1/2 cups chili sauce
1 tablespoon brown sugar
1 tablespoon mustard
1 tablespoon freshly squeezed lemon juice
2 garlic cloves, minced

Combine eggs, turkey, bread crumbs, onion, garlic, parsley, ketchup, soy sauce, salt, and pepper. Form into 1-inch balls. Place balls on an ungreased baking sheet with 1-inch sides. Bake, uncovered, at 450° for 8 to 10 minutes, or until turkey is no longer pink. Drain as necessary.

Meanwhile, in a slow cooker, mix together cranberry sauce, chili sauce, sugar, mustard, lemon juice, and garlic. Stir well over low setting. Add cooked turkey rounds to cranberry mixture in slow cooker. Stir well to coat with sauce. Cover with lid and cook on low setting for 2 hours, stirring occasionally. Serve warm.

This recipe used by permission of the National Turkey Federation.

TURKEY BREAST

1 (2 to 3-1/2-pound) frozen turkey breast, thawed
1/2 cup orange juice
1/2 cup water
1 teaspoon dried rosemary
1/2 teaspoon dried thyme
1/8 cup sugar

Place frozen turkey breast in a slow cooker. Pour remaining ingredients on top. Cover and cook on low for 7 to 8 hours.

TURKEY STUFFING

1 cup butter
2 cups onion, chopped
2 cups celery, chopped
1/4 cup parsley, chopped
2 (8-ounce) cans mushrooms
12 cups bread cubes, day old
1 teaspoon poultry seasoning
1-1/2 teaspoons sage
1 teaspoon thyme
1/2 teaspoon pepper
1/4 teaspoon garlic powder
3-1/2 cups chicken or turkey broth
2 eggs, well beaten

Melt butter in a skillet and sauté onion, celery, parsley, and mushrooms. Pour over bread cubes in a very large mixing bowl. Add all seasonings and toss well. Pour in enough broth to moisten. Add eggs and mix well. Pack lightly into a slow cooker. Cover and cook on low 6 to 8 hours. Makes 12 servings.

Italian Turkey Sandwiches

1 pound Italian turkey sausage
1-1/2 pounds ground turkey
1 large sweet onion, thinly sliced
2 large green bell peppers, seeded and chopped
2 large red bell peppers, seeded and chopped
1 teaspoon salt
1 teaspoon black pepper
1/4 teaspoon red pepper flakes
10 hoagie rolls, split
1-1/4 pounds Provolone cheese, grated

Squeeze sausage out of the casings into a large heavy skillet. Over medium heat, brown sausage and ground turkey, breaking up sausage and ground turkey into medium pieces. Cook until sausage is no longer pink. Remove from skillet with a slotted spoon and reserve. In a bowl, toss vegetables together with salt, pepper, and red pepper flakes. Place one-third of the vegetable mixture in a slow cooker. Layer one-half of the turkey mixture atop the vegetables. Repeat layers of raw vegetables and browned turkey, ending with a top layer of vegetables. Cover and cook on low for 6 hours or until the vegetables are tender. Serve on split hoagie rolls. Sprinkle each sandwich with Provolone cheese.

This recipe used by permission of the National Turkey Federation.

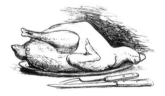

HERBED TURKEY CUTLETS

2 pounds turkey cutlets, cut into 1/3-pound portions
1/2 teaspoon salt
1/2 teaspoon freshly ground black pepper
2 tablespoons unsalted butter
1 medium onion, thinly sliced
4 ounces button mushrooms, cleaned and sliced
1/2 cup chicken broth
1/2 teaspoon dried oregano
1/2 teaspoon dried thyme
cooked rice

Pat turkey cutlets dry with a clean paper towel. Sprinkle both sides with salt and pepper.

Over medium-high heat, melt butter in a hot skillet. Add turkey cutlets and quickly brown both sides. With a slotted spoon, transfer cutlets to slow cooker. Sauté onion and mushrooms in hot skillet until vegetables are soft. Reduce heat and add broth. Simmer for 10 to 15 minutes. Pour mixture over turkey. Sprinkle with herbs. Cover and cook on low setting for 6 to 8 hours or on high setting for 2-1/2 to 3 hours. Serve turkey cutlets over cooked rice with juice from the pot.

This recipe used by permission of the National Turkey Federation.

TURKEY ROAST WITH VEGETABLES

non-stick cooking spray
1 cup onion, chopped
3 cups red potato, diced
1 pound fresh baby carrots
1 (10-3/4-ounce) can condensed cream of celery soup
1/2 cup cold water
1 teaspoon poultry seasoning
1/4 teaspoon salt
3 pounds boneless turkey breast roast, thawed if frozen
1 tablespoon no-salt seasoning blend
1/4 cup instant mashed potato flakes
fresh parsley leaves, chopped fine

Coat a slow cooker with no-stick cooking spray. Place onion, potato, and carrots in slow cooker turned onto low setting. Stir together soup, water, poultry seasoning, and salt. Pour over vegetables. Pat turkey breast roast dry with clean paper towels. Lift string netting and shift position on roast for easier removal after cooking. Sprinkle seasoning blend over roast and place roast on vegetables. Cover; cook on low setting for 6 to 8 hours or until the internal temperature registers 170°. Remove roast from slow cooker. Let stand 10 minutes. Meanwhile, stir potato flakes and parsley into vegetables. Let stand 5 minutes. Remove string netting and cut roast into slices. Serve turkey with vegetables.

This recipe used by permission of the National Turkey Federation.

Barbecue Turkey Sandwich

2 cups cooked turkey, skin removed
1/2 cup white vinegar
1/2 cup ketchup
2 teaspoons Worcestershire sauce
2 teaspoons freshly ground black pepper
1 teaspoon hot pepper sauce
1/2 teaspoon salt
1 lemon, quartered
4 burger buns, split horizontally and toasted

Cut turkey from bones and cut into strips or cubes. Cover and reserve in refrigerator.

In a slow cooker set on high, combine vinegar, ketchup, Worcestershire sauce, pepper, hot sauce, salt, and lemon quarters. Fold in cooked turkey pieces. Cover and cook on high for 4 to 5 hours or on low for 8 to 9 hours. Remove lemon quarters. To serve, spoon hot barbecue mixture over bottom half of toasted burger buns. Top with other half.

This recipe used by permission of the National Turkey Federation.

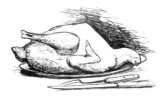

HUNTER'S TURKEY

1 large green bell pepper, seeded and chopped
1 cup sweet onions, sliced
2 celery stalks, chopped into 1/4-inch slices
8 ounces fresh mushrooms, cleaned and sliced
2 pounds turkey cutlets, cut into 5-ounce portions
1/8 teaspoon garlic salt
1/2 teaspoon pepper
1/4 teaspoon ground cinnamon
1/4 cup chicken broth
1 (15-ounce) can crushed tomatoes
3 tablespoons flour
3 tablespoons cold water
pasta, cooked and drained

Place vegetables in slow cooker set on low. Sprinkle both sides of each turkey cutlet with garlic salt, pepper, and cinnamon. Layer cutlets atop vegetables. Add broth and tomatoes. Stir well to combine all ingredients. Cover and cook on low for 7 to 10 hours or on high for 2 to 3 hours. Make a smooth paste of flour and water. Stir into ingredients, blending well. Cover and cook on high setting for 20 to 25 minutes or until the sauce has thickened. Ladle atop cooked pasta.

This recipe used by permission of the National Turkey Federation.

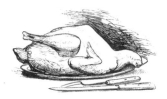

TURKEY NACHOS

3 pounds turkey thighs
1 (1-1/4-ounce) package taco seasoning mix
1 (14-1/2-ounce) can diced tomatoes, with juices
1 (15-ounce) can pinto beans
1 (4-1/2-ounce) can green chilies, chopped
1 teaspoon dried oregano
1/2 teaspoon cumin
2 tablespoons fresh lime juice
white corn tortilla chips
1 cup jalapeño cheese, shredded
1 cup red bell pepper, seeded and chopped fine
1/4 cup black olives, well drained
1/4 cup green onions, chopped
2/3 cup sour cream
1/4 cup fresh cilantro sprigs
2/3 cup salsa
10 lime wedges, seeds removed

Remove bones and skin from turkey thighs. Place thighs in a slow cooker. Sprinkle thighs with taco seasoning mix. Cover with tomatoes, beans, chilies, oregano, cumin, and lime juice. Set cooker on low setting and cover. Cook for 7 to 8 hours.

Remove turkey thighs from cooker and allow to slightly cool. Shred into thin strips. Mash beans with tomatoes, chilies, and herbs. Return turkey to slow cooker and blend all together. Continue to heat on low setting for up to 2 hours.

Place tortillas on large oven-proof platter. Spoon turkey mixture onto tortillas. Sprinkle each with cheese, red peppers, olives, and onions. Heat at 425° for about 5 minutes, or until cheese melts. Serve with sour cream, cilantro, salsa, and lime.

This recipe used by permission of the National Turkey Federation.

MEXICAN TURKEY

2 dried ancho chilies
2 cups boiling water
1 tablespoon vegetable oil
2-1/2 pounds turkey breast, skin on
2 medium onions, sliced
3 garlic cloves, sliced
2 serrano chilies, chopped
4 whole cloves
1 tablespoon chili powder
1/4 teaspoon ground cinnamon
1 teaspoon salt
1 teaspoon black peppercorns, crushed
1 (28-ounce) can tomatillos, drained
1/2 cup whole blanched almonds
1 ounce unsweetened chocolate, broken into pieces
1/4 cup cilantro, finely chopped
3 tablespoons mild green chilies, diced

In a heat-proof bowl, soak dried ancho chilies in boiling water for 30 minutes, making sure all parts of the pepper are submerged. Drain and discard water. Coarsely chop chili and set aside.

In a skillet, heat oil over medium-high heat. Add turkey breast and brown on both sides. Transfer to slow cooker stoneware.

Reduce skillet temperature to medium heat. Add onions to pan and cook, stirring, until softened. Stir in ancho chilies, garlic, serrano chilies, cloves, chili powder, cinnamon, salt, and pepper. Cook, stirring, for 1 minute. Transfer mixture to a food processor. Add tomatillos, almonds, and chocolate, and process until smooth. Pour sauce over turkey, cover and cook on high for 4 hours or on low for 8 hours, or until the internal temperature of the turkey reaches 170°. Garnish with chopped cilantro and diced green chilies.

This recipe used by permission of the National Turkey Federation.

THREE INGREDIENT TURKEY

1 frozen turkey breast, thawed
1 pound can cranberry sauce
1 package dry onion soup mix

Put all ingredients into a slow cooker, cover, and cook for 2 hours on high. Then reduce heat to low and continue cooking for 4 to 5 hours, until turkey registers 180 ° on an instant meat thermometer. Slice turkey breast and serve with sauce.

TURKEY PARMESAN MEATBALLS

1-1/2 pounds ground turkey
1/4 cup pesto sauce
1 teaspoon hot pepper flakes
1/3 cup Parmesan cheese, grated
1 sweet onion, minced
1/2 teaspoon salt
2 teaspoons vegetable oil
2 (28-ounce) cans diced tomatoes
1 tablespoon pesto sauce
1 (5-1/2-ounce) can tomato paste
1 teaspoon granulated sugar
1/4 cup beef stock
hot cooked pasta

In a large bowl, combine ground turkey, 1/4 cup pesto, hot pepper flakes, Parmesan cheese, onion, and salt. Shape mixture into thirty 1-1/2-inch balls. In a large non-stick skillet, heat oil. Place meatballs in skillet, cook 1 to 2 minutes per side, until lightly browned.

Place meatballs in slow cooker. Add diced tomatoes, pesto sauce, tomato paste, sugar, and beef stock. Stir carefully to combine. Cook on high for 4 to 6 hours, or until meatballs are cooked through. Serve over hot cooked pasta.

TURKEY DIJON

1 fresh bone-in turkey breast
3 tablespoons Dijon mustard
2/3 cup 100% fruit juice
1 teaspoon salt
1/8 teaspoon pepper

Put turkey breast, skin side up, in a slow cooker. Spread with Dijon mustard and season with salt and pepper . Pour juice over the turkey and cover the slow cooker. Cook on low 8 to 9 hours, until turkey is tender and thoroughly cooked.

WILD RICE-STUFFED TURKEY

1-1/2 cups wild rice
1 onion, finely chopped
1/2 cup dried cranberries
2 apples, chopped
3 cups water
4 to 5 pounds boneless whole turkey breast, thawed if frozen

Mix rice, onion, dried cranberries and apples; place in bottom of a slow cooker. Pour water over, making sure all wild rice is submerged. Place turkey on top of rice mixture.

Cover and cook on low for 8 to 9 hours, or until turkey is thoroughly cooked and reaches 180° on a meat thermometer, and wild rice is tender. Makes 10 servings.

SEAFOOD

POACHED SALMON

1 pound salmon fillets
1/2 cup onion, sliced
2 fresh thyme sprigs
1 bay leaf
1/2 teaspoon salt
1/4 teaspoon pepper
3/4 cup water
1/4 cup chicken broth
1 tablespoon fresh lemon juice

Place the salmon fillets in the bottom of a slow cooker. Top with remaining ingredients. Cover and cook on low for 2 to 3 hours, or until salmon flakes easily with a fork.

BAKED SALMON

2 (16-ounce) cans salmon
4 cups bread crumbs
1 teaspoon fresh lemon juice
1 green bell pepper, chopped
1 cup boiling water
4 eggs, well beaten
1 teaspoon garlic powder
1 teaspoon Greek seasoning
1/4 teaspoon dry mustard
1 teaspoon dill weed, finely chopped
2 chicken bouillon cubes

In a well-greased slow cooker, combine all of the ingredients. Cover and cook on high for 4 to 5 hours.

SWISS CRAB CASSEROLE

4 tablespoons butter
1 medium onion, chopped
1/2 green bell pepper, chopped
1/4 cup celery, chopped
4 tablespoons flour
2-1/2 cups crab or shrimp stock
1 cup rice
2 cups crabmeat
2 cups Swiss cheese, shredded
1 cup mushrooms, sliced
1 cup bread crumbs
1/2 cup Swiss cheese, shredded

In a large saucepan, melt the butter over medium heat. Add the celery, onion, and bell pepper, and sauté until tender, about 3 to 5 minutes. Stir in flour and stock, and bring to a boil. Cook until slightly thickened, about 2 minutes.

In a slow cooker, combine crabmeat, 2 cups Swiss cheese, and mushrooms. Pour in sauce and stir lightly. Cover and cook on high for 3 to 5 hours.

Pour into a casserole and cover with cracker crumbs. Sprinkle 1/2 cup Swiss cheese on top and put under a broiler until cheese melts.

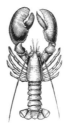

TUNA CASSEROLE

2 (10-ounce) cans cream of chicken soup
1 cup milk
2 (7-ounce) cans tuna, drained
1/2 cup onion, chopped
1 cup frozen peas
1-1/2 cups elbow macaroni, cooked
1 cup mushrooms, sliced

In a small bowl, mix together the soup and milk. Pour into a slow cooker along with the rest of the ingredients. Cover and cook on high for 3 to 4 hours.

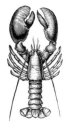

SHRIMP CREOLE

2 tablespoons butter
1 cup celery, diced
1 cup onion, chopped
1 cup green bell pepper, chopped
1 garlic clove, minced
1 (6-ounce) can tomato paste
1 (28-ounce) can whole tomatoes
1 cup water
1 bay leaf
1 teaspoon salt
1/4 teaspoon pepper
2 teaspoons hot sauce
2 pounds shrimp, peeled and deveined
rice, cooked

In a skillet, melt the butter over medium heat. Sauté celery, onion, bell pepper, and onion in butter until soft, about 2 to 3 minutes. Pour into a slow cooker along with tomato paste, tomatoes, water, bay leaf, salt, pepper, and hot sauce. Cover and cook on high 3 to 4 hours. Add shrimp the last hour of cooking. Serve with rice.

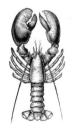

CARIBBEAN SHRIMP

1 pound shrimp, peeled and deveined
1 teaspoon orange zest
1/4 cup orange juice
1/4 cup lime juice
1 teaspoon brown sugar
2 garlic cloves, minced
1 teaspoon chili powder
1/2 teaspoon dried oregano
1 teaspoon salt
1 cup frozen peas
1 tomato, diced
cooked rice

In a slow cooker, combine the shrimp, orange zest, juices, brown sugar, garlic, chili powder oregano, and salt. Cover and cook on low for 2 hours. Stir in peas and tomatoes, increase heat to high, and cook covered for 10 more minutes. Serve over rice.

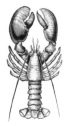

CURRIED SHRIMP

1 pound shrimp, peeled and deveined
2 garlic cloves, minced
2 tablespoons ginger, grated
1 onion, chopped
1 red bell pepper, chopped
1-1/2 teaspoons salt
1 teaspoon pepper
1 tablespoon curry powder
1 (13-ounce) can coconut milk
1/4 cup fresh lime juice
rice, cooked
cilantro, chopped

In a slow cooker, combine shrimp, garlic, ginger, onion, bell pepper, salt, pepper, curry powder, coconut milk, and lime juice. Cover and cook on low 4 to 6 hours. Serve over rice garnished with cilantro.

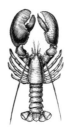

SHRIMP MARINARA

1 (28-ounce) can chopped tomatoes
1 (6-ounce) can tomato paste
1 onion, finely chopped
1 garlic clove, minced
1 tablespoon fresh basil, chopped
1 teaspoon dried oregano
1/2 teaspoon salt
1/4 teaspoon pepper
1/2 teaspoon sugar
1 pound shrimp, peeled and deveined
1/4 cup Parmesan cheese, grated
2 cups spaghetti, cooked

In a slow cooker, combine the tomatoes, tomato paste, onion, garlic, basil, oregano, salt, pepper, and sugar. Cover and cook on low for 6 to 7 hours. Add the shrimp the last hour of cooking. Serve over spaghetti topped with cheese.

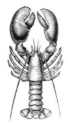

CHOW MEIN CASSEROLE

1 can mushroom soup
1 small green pepper, chopped
1 cup celery, chopped
1 can tuna fish in spring water, drained
1/4 cup milk
1/4 cup onion, chopped
1 cup chow mein noodles

Mix all ingredients except chow mein noodles in a slow cooker. Cover and cook on low for 7 to 8 hours. Add chow mein noodles during the last hour of cooking.

SEAFOOD NEWBURG

1 tablespoon butter
1/2 cup onion, chopped
1/2 cup green bell pepper, chopped
2 (10-ounce) cans cream of shrimp soup
1-1/2 cups milk
1 pound shrimp, cooked
1 cup lobster tail meat, cooked and chopped
1-1/2 cups lump crab meat
1 tablespoon paprika
1 teaspoon salt
1/2 teaspoon pepper
rice, cooked

In a skillet, melt the butter over medium heat. Add the onion and bell pepper, and sauté until tender, 2 to 3 minutes. Pour into a slow cooker along with the rest of the ingredients. Cover and cook on low for 4 to 6 hours. Serve with rice.

SNAPPER VERA CRUZ

1 tablespoon olive oil
1 large onion, finely chopped
2 garlic cloves, minced
1/2 teaspoon dried oregano
1 teaspoon cilantro, chopped
1/4 teaspoon sugar
1/4 teaspoon cumin
2 jalapeño peppers, finely chopped
1 can (28-ounce) diced peeled tomatoes, drained
1/2 cup fish stock
4 (8 to 10-ounce) snapper fillets, butterflied
salt and pepper, to taste
2 tablespoons lemon juice
1 tablespoon capers
1 small jar green olives, sliced

In a skillet, heat oil over medium heat. Sauté onion until softened. Add garlic, oregano, cilantro, sugar, cumin, and jalapeño peppers. Sauté until fragrant, about 1 minute. Add the tomatoes and stock and bring to a boil.

Transfer to a slow cooker. Cover and cook on high for 3 to 4 hours. Season the fish fillets with salt and pepper, then add to slow cooker with lemon juice. Cover and continue cooking until fish is done, about 20 minutes. Stir in capers and green olives; serve.

SCALLOPED OYSTERS

1 quart oysters
2 cups saltine cracker crumbs
1-1/2 cups bread crumbs
2/3 cup Parmesan cheese, grated
3/4 cups butter, melted
2 eggs, beaten
salt and pepper, to taste

In a large bowl, combine all the ingredients and mix well. Pour into a greased slow cooker. Cover and cook on low for 5 to 6 hours.

FISH AU GRATIN

6 tablespoons butter
3 tablespoons flour
1-1/2 teaspoons salt
1 teaspoon pepper
1-1/2 cups milk
1 tablespoon lemon juice
1 cup Parmesan cheese, grated
3 pounds white fish fillets
2 tablespoons green onion, chopped

In a skillet, melt butter over medium heat. Add flour, salt, and pepper; stir. Slowly add milk, stirring constantly until thickened. Add lemon juice and cheese. Put fish fillets into a slow cooker. Pour sauce over fish. Cover and cook on high for 1 to 2 hours, or until fish is cooked through. Serve garnished with green onion.

Salmon Loaf

1 (16-ounce) can salmon
2 eggs, beaten
1-1/2 cups soft bread crumbs
1/4 cup onion, finely chopped
2 tablespoon butter or margarine
1 tablespoon snipped parsley
1 tablespoon lemon juice
1/4 teaspoon salt
dash of cayenne pepper
1/2 cup sharp cheddar cheese, shredded

Drain salmon, reserve juices. Combine juices with remaining ingredients except the salmon and cheese. Flake salmon; stir into mixture. Shape into round loaf. Line the slow cooker with aluminum foil to come up 2 to 3-inches on sides. Place loaf on foil, not touching sides. Cover and cook on low for 4 to 5 hours. Add the cheese the last 5 minutes of cooking.

DESSERTS

Chocolate Applesauce Cake

1-1/2 cups all-purpose flour
2 teaspoons baking soda
1 teaspoon baking powder
1/8 teaspoon salt
1/4 cup plus 2 tablespoons unsalted butter
1 cup sugar
1 cup unsweetened applesauce
1 teaspoon cinnamon
1 teaspoon vanilla extract
3 eggs
1/4 pound unsweetened chocolate, melted
1/3 cup buttermilk
3/4 cup semisweet chocolate chips
1/2 cup walnuts, chopped
1/4 cup powdered sugar

Sift first four ingredients together in a bowl. Set aside. Combine butter and sugar in a mixing bowl. Beat with an electric mixer until fluffy. Add next four ingredients and mix thoroughly. With mixer running, pour in melted chocolate and mix thoroughly. Add flour mixture and mix on low speed until just blended. Slowly beat in buttermilk. Stir in chocolate chips and walnuts.

Transfer batter to a slow cooker on high heat. Smooth top. Cover and cook 2-1/4 to 2-1/2 hours, or until a tester comes out clean when inserted into center. Remove lid, turn off cooker, and let cake cool in cooker until just barely warm. Run a sharp knife around inside edges of cooker. Use a large spatula to carefully remove cake in one piece. Sprinkle with powdered sugar before serving.

APPLE PIE

8 tart apples, peeled and sliced
1-1/4 teaspoons ground cinnamon
1/4 teaspoon allspice
1/4 teaspoon nutmeg
3/4 cup milk
2 tablespoons butter, softened
3/4 cup sugar
2 eggs
2 teaspoons vanilla
1-1/2 cups Bisquick, divided
1/3 cup brown sugar
3 tablespoons butter, cold

Toss apples in a large bowl with cinnamon, allspice, and nutmeg. Place apple mixture in a lightly greased slow cooker. Combine milk, softened butter, sugar, eggs, vanilla, and 1/2 cup of the Bisquick. Spoon over apples.

Combine the remaining Bisquick with the brown sugar. Cut cold butter into Bisquick mixture until crumbly. Sprinkle this mixture over top of apple mixture. Cover and cook on low 6 to 7 hours, or until apples are soft.

INDIAN PUDDING

1 cup yellow cornmeal
1/2 cup molasses
1/4 cup sugar
1/4 cup butter
1/4 teaspoon salt
1/4 teaspoon baking soda
2 eggs
6 cups hot milk, divided

In a saucepan, combine all ingredients with 3 cups of the milk. Bring to a simmer. Stir in remaining milk then transfer to a slow cooker. Cover and cook on low for 5 to 7 hours.

CARAMEL RICE PUDDING

3 cups cooked white rice
1/2 cup raisins
2 teaspoons vanilla extract
1 (14-ounce) can sweetened condensed milk
1 (12-ounce) can evaporated milk
1 tablespoon sugar
1 teaspoon ground cinnamon

Prepare the inside of a slow cooker with cooking spray. Mix all ingredients except sugar and cinnamon in the cooker. Cover and cook on low 3 to 4 hours, or until liquid is absorbed. Stir pudding before serving. Sprinkle pudding with sugar and cinnamon. Serve warm. Makes 8 servings.

Streusel Cake

1 (16-ounce) package pound cake mix
1/4 cup brown sugar
1 tablespoon flour
1/4 cup nuts, finely chopped
1 teaspoon cinnamon

Mix cake mix according to directions on package. Liberally grease and flour a 2-pound coffee tin. Pour cake batter into a coffee tin. Mix brown sugar, flour, nuts, and cinnamon together. Sprinkle over top of cake mix. Place coffee tin in slow cooker. Cover with several layers of paper towels. Cover slow cooker and cook on high for 3 to 4 hours.

Cherry Chocolate Dessert

1 (21-ounce) can cherry pie filling
1 package chocolate cake mix
1/2 cup butter melted

Place pie filling in a slow cooker. Combine dry cake mix and butter. Sprinkle over filling. Cover and cook on low for 3 hours. Makes 10 to 12 servings.

BANANA NUT BREAD

1-1/2 cups sugar
1/2 cup butter
2 eggs
1 teaspoon baking soda
4 small ripe bananas, mashed
3 tablespoons water or milk
2 cups flour
1/2 cup pecans, chopped

Cream sugar and butter. Beat in eggs one at a time. Add milk and bananas. Thoroughly mix in remaining ingredients. Pour into a greased 2-pound coffee can. Place in a slow cooker. Cook 3 hours on high.

BAKED APPLES

8 red apples, cored but not peeled
1-1/4 cups brown sugar
4 tablespoons cinnamon
1/2 cup raisins
1-1/2 tablespoons orange zest
1/3 cup butter
2-1/2 cups very hot water

In a buttered pan, place the apples standing up. In a small bowl, mix together the brown sugar, cinnamon, raisins, and orange zest. Fill the apples with this mixture. Place the pan in a slow cooker and pour hot water around it. Cover and cook on low for 3 to 5 hours, or until apples are tender.

BLUEBERRY DUMP CAKE

4 cups fresh blueberries
1/2 cup sugar
1 (18-1/2-ounce) package yellow cake mix
1/2 cup butter, melted
vanilla ice cream

In a small bowl, mix together the blueberries and sugar. Pour into a slow cooker. Combine the cake mix and butter, and pour over the blueberries. Cover and cook on low for 2 to 3 hours. Serve with ice cream.

TRIPLE CHOCOLATE MESS

non-stick cooking spray
1 package chocolate cake mix
2 cups sour cream
1 package instant chocolate pudding
1 (8-ounce) bag chocolate chips
3/4 cup vegetable oil
4 eggs
1 cup water

Coat inside of a slow cooker with cooking spray. In a large bowl, combine all the ingredients and mix thoroughly. Pour the batter into the slow cooker. Cover and cook on low for 5 to 6 hours.

PUMPKIN CHOCOLATE MARBLE CHEESECAKE

1-1/2 cups gingersnap cookies, crumbled
1/2 cup pecans, finely chopped
3 tablespoons light brown sugar
1/3 cup butter, melted
2 (8-ounce) packages cream cheese, softened
3/4 cup sugar
1 teaspoon vanilla
3 eggs
3/4 teaspoon cinnamon
1/4 teaspoon nutmeg
1 (15-ounce) can pumpkin
1/2 cup whipping cream
4 ounces semisweet chocolate, melted
very hot water

In a large bowl, combine the cookie crumbs, pecans, brown sugar, and melted butter. Mix thoroughly. Press into a greased 7-inch springform pan and put in the freezer for at least 30 minutes.

In the bowl of an electric mixer, combine cream cheese, sugar, and vanilla. Mix to combine. Add eggs one at a time, mixing thoroughly after each addition. While mixer is running, add cinnamon, nutmeg, pumpkin, and whipping cream. Pour batter into the pie shell and top with melted chocolate. Gently insert a knife or fork into the pie and slowly make circular motions to create the marbling effect. Cover pie with aluminum foil.

Place pie in a slow cooker and pour hot water around it, enough to fill the slow cooker about 1 inch. Cover and cook on high for 3 to 4 hours. Remove from slow cooker and place in a refrigerator; chill for at least 2 hours before serving.

BANANAS FOSTER

1/2 cup butter
1/2 cup brown sugar
6 bananas, peeled and sliced
1/2 teaspoon vanilla extract
1 tablespoon cinnamon
vanilla ice cream

Melt butter in a slow cooker over low heat. Slowly mix in brown sugar. Add the bananas, vanilla extract, and cinnamon, and cook on low for 1 hour. Serve over vanilla ice cream.

APPLE SLUMP WITH DUMPLINGS

6 apples, peeled, cored, and sliced
1/2 cup apple juice
1/2 cup brown sugar
1 teaspoon cinnamon
1/4 teaspoon nutmeg
pinch of salt
1 cup flour
1-1/2 teaspoons baking powder
1/2 teaspoon salt
1/2 cup sugar
1 egg, beaten
1/2 cup milk
1/2 cup butter, melted
whipped cream

In a slow cooker, combine apples, juice, brown sugar, cinnamon, nutmeg, and a pinch of salt. Cover and cook on low for 4 hours.

When the apples are almost done, sift together the flour, baking powder, sugar, and salt. In a separate bowl, whisk together the egg, milk, and melted butter. Combine the wet and dry ingredients and mix thoroughly. Drop by tablespoonfuls into the slow cooker. Cover and cook on high for 45 more minutes. Serve topped with whipped cream.

CHERRY COBBLER

2 (21-ounce) cans cherry pie filling
1 package yellow cake mix
1/3 cup sugar
1/2 teaspoon cinnamon
1/4 cup butter, melted

Pour pie filling into a slow cooker. In a large bowl, mix together the yellow cake mix, sugar, cinnamon, and butter. Pour over pie filling. Cover and cook on low for 3 to 4 hours.

RICE PUDDING

1 cup uncooked white rice
1 cup sugar
2 (12-ounce) cans evaporated milk
1 teaspoon vanilla extract
1 teaspoon ground cinnamon
1 teaspoon ground nutmeg

Combine all the ingredients in a slow cooker. Cover and cook on low for 1-1/2 hours, stirring occasionally.

LEMON PUDDING CAKE

3 eggs, separated
1/4 cup lemon juice
1 tablespoon lemon peel, grated
3 tablespoons butter
1/8 teaspoon salt
1-1/2 cups milk
3/4 cup sugar
1/4 cup flour

In a small bowl, beat egg whites until stiff peaks form. In another bowl, beat egg yolks, then slowly stir in lemon juice, butter, and milk. Sift together sugar, flour, and salt; add to egg yolk mixture, beating until smooth. Stir in egg whites and pour into a slow cooker. Cover and cook on low 4 to 6 hours.

INDEX

INDEX

INDEX

C

INDEX

INDEX

D

INDEX

E

F

G

INDEX

H

I

J

K

L

M

O

P

INDEX

INDEX

R

INDEX

T

V

INDEX

W

Y